M

BAD MOON RISING

To Michel Marian
Homme d'Esprit

semper fidelis

Gilles Kepel

BAD MOON RISING

A Chronicle of the Middle East Today

Translated from the French by
Pascale Ghazaleh

SAQI

British Library Cataloguing-in-Publication Data
A catalogue record for this book is available from the
British Library

ISBN 0 86356 303 1

Originally published as *Chronique d'une guerre d'Orient*
© Editions Gallimard, Paris 2002

This edition first published 2003 by Saqi Books

The book is supported by the French Ministry for Foreign Affairs, as part of
the Burgess Programme headed for the French Embassy in London by the
Institut Français du Royaume-Uni.

The book is published with the co-operation of the Ministère français
chargé de la culture – Centre national du livre.

Saqi Books
26 Westbourne Grove
London W2 5RH

www.saqibooks.com

Contents

Chronicle of an Oriental War

Saturday 13 October 2001

I had not been back to Cairo in four years. As the evening flight glides over the city before landing, I recognize the streets of Heliopolis: the luminous Arabic sign of Omar Effendi, the department store; the green neon lights hung on minarets, whose night-time presence can only be guessed. I shall cross the airport's threshold, and a breeze laden with the particular perfumes of this land will strike me, a fleeting impression that familiarity will soon dispel. Egypt unfurls its seasons according to an intimate olfactory calendar, bound up since eternity with the ebb and flow of the Nile. Whenever I returned from abroad, tasting the air, eyes closed, I could distinguish between spring and autumn, and knew without fail that I had arrived. Egypt is smelled. The great feast that brings Muslims and Christians together, when spring returns, is called Shamm al-Nissim – 'sniff the breeze'. Only radical Islamists boycott it: it would distract believers from the exclusive adoration of God. But even their curses cannot stop the month when the fragrance of crushed sugar cane fills the air, nor the preceding months of guavas and their suffocating perfume, of ripe mangoes, of the fresh alfalfa that drives the water buffaloes wild. I try in vain to remember which aromatic gust will envelop me in its eddies when I emerge from the airport on this warm evening. I've been away too long.

I notice no apparent deployment of security forces in the arrival hall, despite Bin Laden and all the tension of the Middle East one imagines from Paris. I am out so soon indeed that my friend Abu Skandar, who has factored in plenty of time for customs and police formalities, is not yet there, and I remain alone in the night, smelling an odour I do not recognize. The air, saturated with petrol fumes, is thick with a sort of gray fog; it makes haloes around the headlights of the old Polonez, which arrives at last, and into which I climb. This smell was unknown before, my friend explains; this is the heavy, oppressive smoke from the burning of rice straw. Agriculture was liberalized three years ago in the Nile Delta, and the *fellah*s fell upon the profitable planting of rice. Then they burn the straw, to plant in its stead fava beans, clover, wheat. Government prohibitions, the straw-compacting machines they were offered – they care nothing for these. And every autumn they calmly asphyxiate the city's inhabitants. We spend entire days in this gray, sickly sweet mist that makes Cairo resemble a ghost city, waiting until the peasants are done.

The house where Abu Skandar lives is lit up with a garland of multicolored electric bulbs that punch holes in this warm fog. A police general is giving his daughter away, and on the stairs we meet captains, budding bellies belted in their uniforms' white shirts, walkie-talkies in hand, accompanied by carefully made-up wives, most with a scarf over their hair. The sound system howls popular tunes. The hit of the year, since the beginning of the Palestinian Intifada, is *Ana Bakrah Isra'il* – 'I Hate Israel'. In another grammatical form, this same Arabic verb, *karaha*, 'to hate', signifies 'to coerce'. It lies at the heart of a Qur'anic verse regularly quoted at ecumenical encounters with believers of other faiths: '*la ikrah fi'l-din*' – 'there is no compulsion in religion'. But in the planetary drama that has been playing since the World Trade Center was destroyed on 11 September 2001, and Bin Laden and his protectors implicated, perhaps religion is only the crystallization of far larger conflicts: the language in which to express, for lack of a better alternative, the vast disquiet in the civilization of Muslim societies, the relation – both intimate and conflicted – in which they are intertwined with the Western world.

At dawn, a loudspeaker affixed to a nearby wall wakes me with a start, flinging out the call to prayer, the volume turned up all the way, saturated by static. I had forgotten the *muezzin*. In two or three nights, like everybody else, I will have integrated it into sleep. I will hear it no longer.

11

Sunday 14 October

The headlines of the three main dailies, which reflect the regime's views, strike an approximate balance between denunciations of terrorism and of the bombing of civilians in Afghanistan, thus humouring both the great American ally – which doles out about two billion dollars in vital aid to Egypt every year – and popular sentiment. But most of the pages these days are devoted to celebrating President Mubarak's twenty years in power. *Al-Akhbar* ('The News') carries a special supplement, abundantly illustrated, that sings the *rayyis*'s praises in every possible field. Commercial firms compete with full-page ads congratulating him. Dignitaries and deputies, military men and academics, engineers and physicians, agriculturalists, women or journalists: all cough up panegyrics celebrating his achievements in their respective fields.

Twenty years ago, on 6 October 1981, during a parade held to commemorate the October 1973 War, Anwar Sadat was assassinated by Islamist militants belonging to the al-Jihad ('holy war') group. Mubarak, his vice-president, who suffered only an injured hand in the assault, became his successor. Several hundred imprisoned activists were then freed in 1984 and encouraged to leave Egypt via the pilgrimage to Mecca, so that they could continue their *jihad* in Afghanistan against the Red Army under the auspices of Saudi Arabia and the CIA, who were financing the war against Communist atheism. For Egyptian officials, this was a boon: the most extremist beards were clearing out, going off to fight in the service of the American ally, and if, perchance, they happened to die, it had been divinely ordained ... History's ruses were to foil these too skilful plans, and the same beards, now hardened by war, would return to shake the regime with a wide-scale terrorist offensive between 1992 and 1997. Today, one of these outcasts, an Egyptian physician named Ayman al-Zawahiri, the scion of an important family, is seated at Bin Laden's side on the videotapes that are touring the world thanks to the satellite TV station al-Jazeera.

In that autumn of 1981 I lived in Cairo, where I was writing my dissertation on the Islamist movements from which Sadat's assassins were to emerge. I remember the day the *rayyis* was killed very precisely. The young woman who worked for me, a lively and engaging peasant married to a motorcyclist in the police force, suddenly came running back just after she had finished work, at around three in the afternoon. I had never seen her so overexcited. 'Mr Gilles ,' she said in dialect, 'they've shot Sadat! *In sha'Allah mawwituh* (God willing, they've killed him)!' And yet, what praise the Western press had heaped on the 'president of peace', who had signed the treaty with Israel! What tributes the courtiers and sycophants who surrounded him had placed at his feet ... Today, only the opposition daily *al-Wafd* ('The Delegation'), published by the party of the same name, ignores the tributes to the president, just as it distances itself from the official line and abstains from drumming up support

13

for the war on terror. Its front page carries photos of wounded Afghan children and anti-American demonstrations in Jakarta and Quetta. The following day, it will publish a long back-page article to condemn the awarding of the Nobel Prize in literature to V. S. Naipaul, and in peace to Kofi Annan, both of whom it denounces as enemies of the Muslims.

Traditionally, the Wafd, which traces its origins back to the First World War, was a secular party headed by moderate notables and bourgeois, where Copts – Egyptian Christians – were well-represented. These days, its daily has taken on an infuriated tenor one would expect more readily from an Islamist paper – but the Muslim Brothers' newspapers are prohibited; the party is ogling that readership, and those voters. Is it the sign of a generalized Islamization of manners and mentalities that some believe is growing ever stronger? The journalistic equivalent of the veils covering the hair of over half the Egyptian women one meets on the street, with a frequency that seems to have stabilized or even regressed slightly since my last sojourn? I go off to ask Gamal al-Ghitani. We have known each other for twenty years. Today, he is considered one of the greatest contemporary Arab writers. To reach his office in the building of the daily *al-Akhbar*, where he heads a supplement called *Akhbar al-Adab* ('Literary News'), one navigates through swarms of ushers and lift operators, through immense rooms where men and women who seem to have nothing to do are sipping tea or coffee. His little office, in contrast, is a constantly buzzing hive where guests and colleagues come and go without a pause, finding seats on black fake-leather chairs among the files and books piled everywhere.

When last I was here, four years ago, he was greeting students from Central Asia, fresh graduates of the unchanged Soviet system, who were writing a thesis on one of his novels. Thrilled, they had posed at the master's side for a photograph taken with their Russian camera before departing. Gamal's entire literary oeuvre seeks to inscribe Arab culture within universal civilization; he has had to struggle against the most conservative religious figures (who had *The Thousand and One Nights* banned for obscenity) and battle the censorship of contemporary novels containing even faintly iconoclastic allusions to Islam. Offhand, he feels no sympathy for Bin Laden and those who share his vision of society. Everyone in his office condemns the 11 September attacks on New York and Washington, the unforgivable terrorist act that claimed the lives of thousands of innocent civilians. But soon reservations are expressed with regard to US policy in the Middle East. The young journalists taking part in the conversation speak of the embargo on Iraq, of how Iraqi society was suffering while Saddam Hussein emerged from the Gulf War stronger than before. They are especially vehement in condemning the US's failure to intervene in the Israeli-Palestinian conflict since the al-Aqsa Intifada began, in autumn of 2000. In the name of anti-imperialism, these same nationalists – or their parents – once railed against the American superpower's interference; today, it

15

is accused of benign neglect, and of allowing the stronger party, Israel, to dominate its Palestinian adversary.

A curious relationship with America and the West in general has developed in our globalized universe: declarations of distrust are combined with a very powerful attraction; rejection of the paradigm with admiration for a democratic system of which most of the Muslim world's societies are still deprived; and claims of cultural specificity with a desire for recognition and the irrepressible wish to participate equally in universal culture. And, failing America, I am asked why Europe does not intervene, why the old colonial powers, intimately acquainted with the societies of the south-eastern Mediterranean, do not play a mediating role to avoid breaches that would have potentially catastrophic consequences for Arabs and Muslims, first and foremost, if Bin Laden or the Taliban managed to capture the popular imagination in any lasting way.

Monday 15 October
Roda Island is a haven of calm in Cairo's clamour. The Muslim Brothers have their headquarters here in a discreet Nile-side apartment. One leaves one's shoes at the door: the vestibule, covered in wall-to-wall carpeting that has known better days, serves as a prayer room, I am told. Perhaps this is also a way of imposing upon visitors the movement's cultural codes, of indicating to the Westerner that, along with shoes, arrogance and certitudes must be left behind. I remember the televised images of Shevardnadze – then Soviet foreign minister –

received in socks by Khomeini, who had granted him an audience.

I have an appointment with Issam al-Erian. Fifty or so, a few years older than me, he is vice-president of the Physicians' Syndicate – one of the first professional organizations to fall under the Brotherhood's control, since its most important student bastions in the 1970s were in the faculties of medicine and engineering. I had translated and presented one of his articles, written when he was in med school, in my dissertation twenty years ago. We met later in Holland, at a conference. He had read the Arabic translation of one of my books, *The Revenge of God*, and had rebuked me for focusing on 'extremists' instead of 'moderates' like him. I had taken note of his remark, and it is partly because of it that I subsequently paid closer attention to the specific claims of the 'pious middle classes' – which provided me with a key to reading contemporary Islamist movements – in their complementarity with, or opposition to, the 'young urban poor'.

He greets me warmly. We begin by evoking the years that have passed since we last met. He spent five years in prison, and asks me if I find him changed. His mustache has gone completely white. The former prisoner has taken a stand in favour of freeing a prisoner of conscience: the Egyptian-American academic Saadeddin Ibrahim, sworn enemy of the Islamists, now victim to the wrath of a regime that nurtured him, fallen from grace after his demands that the last legislative

17

elections take place under international supervision. Officially, Mr Ibrahim was accused of financial misconduct, but the members of his defense team do not believe a word of it. In taking this stand, the Muslim Brother Issam al-Erian, emblematic physician of the pious middle classes, has made a move appreciated by the democrats and secularists. He is reasonably well-informed on the debates taking place among French specialists on the Islamist movements and knows that, unlike certain academics who exalt this cause, which they ingratiatingly perceive as the authenticity of the peoples of the South, I take a more distant view of matters – which does not necessarily incline me towards sympathy for the movement. But for him, this is no doubt an opportunity to convey messages where the Islamists' fellow-travellers have little credibility. He hands me a bundle of communiqués from the Egyptian Muslim Brotherhood and from other organizations or imams linked to them throughout the world, like Sheikh Yusuf al-Qaradawi, whose Sunday programme *al-Shari'a wa-l-Hayat* ('Islamic Law and Life') on al-Jazeera has elevated him to global preaching stardom.

The texts condemn in very strong language the 11 September attacks, described as terrorist acts in total opposition to the message of Islam, and their authors, whoever they may be, of a 'crime against humanity'. The condemnation's virulence is then the pretext for denouncing, with predictably equal vigour 'Zionist terrorism' in Palestine and also opposing any US strike on 'the brotherly Afghan people'. But one would be mistaken to take lightly the condemnation of the attacks on the US. Even if Bin Laden is never mentioned by name, and if US officials are asked to provide proof, the Islamist trend organized around the Brotherhood – which has set itself up as the mouthpiece of the pious middle classes – is mainly afraid of finding itself dragged into a game of one-upmanship it does not control. It fears it would have everything to lose in the sparking of a *jihad* that will ultimately turn against it, inaugurate a long period of uncertainty or even ruination for the populations of the Muslim world, unleash pandemonium which the authoritarian regimes will use to regain the upper hand and repress the Brotherhood by lumping it with the forces of sedition.

Only a few kilometres of traffic jams along the old residential area of Garden City separate Roda Island from the American University in Cairo. Many beautiful colonial villas, belonging to *ancien regime* pashas, Britons, Frenchmen or Jews, were sequestered after the Tripartite Aggression against the Suez Canal in 1956 and then transformed into public buildings. They are dirty, some half-ruined, generally ill-kept, but that has often saved them from demolition in the face of the frenzied speculation that has gripped Cairo real estate in the past twenty years. The American University is an enclave; behind its high walls are the children of the wealthier classes – fees, depending on majors, are around 15,000 euros a year excluding imported textbooks, which are very expensive. And not infrequently, one sees students getting out of beautiful chauffeur-driven cars – while their counterparts at Egypt's public universities are forced to make endless journeys on rickety, jam-packed buses. Indeed, it is by offering students the exclusive use of a minibus network that Islamist militants on campus built their popularity twenty-five years ago, and launched the veil in universities ... At the American University, a visible minority of veiled girls and bearded boys stands out against the crowd of students, among whom tight brand-name jeans dominate along with hairstyles in the manner of American soap operas, reminiscent of shampoo ads.

In the middle of the campus, a large warehouse-shaped building, which clashes with the carefully groomed architecture of the whole, bears the sign 'Praying Ground'; a colleague who had just arrived from Canada and was unaccustomed to finding mosques in the centre of universities first thought it read 'Playing Ground'. It is a mosque, though, and from it the call to prayer suddenly rings out, in the very heart of the principal vector of American cultural influence on Egyptian bourgeois youth. In the bilingual campus weekly, *The Caravan/al-Qafila*, an article by a student notes that 'religion is making progress on campus despite the stereotypes', and that there is nothing wrong with Westernization, as long as it allows one to take from other cultures those aspects beneficial to local society. The American University made headlines a few years ago when parents protested against professors who were assigning their students 'immoral' texts; the administration paid close attention to the complaints of those who were paying such high admission fees, and the heretical books written by Maxime Rodinson or this author, previously available in the library, were consigned to oblivion.

Here one puts one's finger on the entire paradox of relations with the West, and the US in particular: expatriate families get rich and return from the Arabian Peninsula, then send their veiled daughters to the American University rather than to the public universities, deemed excessively 'common'. America fascinates; one may try out immersion in its civilization, culture, modes of consumption; one may make it into a mark of distinction; but one will be sure to negotiate a particular identity within that framework. What is being played out here is not a war of civilizations, but rather an attempt to participate in a globally dominant one, to influence its content and even – for the most militant – to appropriate it.

On Falaki Square behind the American University, in the old colonial quarter now dilapidated and filthy and around the Baltard-style covered market where an obsolete French inscription proclaims 'Bab al-Luq Market', stalls sell satellite dishes of all sizes piled on the pavement. They capture al-Jazeera, but also Arte (its films much appreciated by intellectuals, for it is a unique window onto European culture) as well as American channels and hardcore Turkish porn, which starts late at night. I am told that since 11 September, both demand and prices have exploded on the satellite dish market: supposedly a sign of victory for al-Jazeera. But this also means access to freedom in a world where the regime controls information stringently. Satellite television allows freedom of choice.

Further on is the only popular café where one can still drink a fizzy Stella beer in the long, retro, narrow-necked bottles – even if to do so one must pass behind a screen that isolates one from the street, and sit among tables at which men are conscientiously imbibing local brandy with water. The café is run by Copts – Egyptian Christians, recognizable by the cross tattooed on the inside of their wrist. The indelible ink marks them as so many lambs of God, fragile protection against the pervasiveness of Islam and the pressure to convert to the dominant religion, which the Christian clergy experiences as a permanent threat of plunder against its flock. The previous night, in a restaurant that foreigners frequent, I could not get a beer – it was the commemoration of the Prophet's nocturnal ascension to heaven, the *mi'raj*. The café is called *al-Horriyya* – 'Liberty'. A few years ago I shared a water pipe there with Golo, a French artist who lives in the old quarter of Sakakini, whence he roams the city sketching snapshots of street life and capturing staggeringly truthful scenes that say more about Egypt than many a heavy tome. The honey-steeped tobacco had made us a little dizzy, and we had readily agreed that the name of the café where we were smoking our water pipe, no doubt baptized 'Liberty' in homage to national independence, had taken on a new meaning: the last dive in the neighbourhood where one was free to drink a beer.

The Ministry of Foreign Affairs stands tall, a modern Nile-side tower, across from the palace on the island of Zamalek where the Empress Eugénie stayed in 1869. She came to inaugurate both the Suez Canal and the Cairo Opera, where Verdi had created *Aïda*. This capitalist graft on Egypt's vigorous body was to bear bittersweet fruits. Today, the palace's outmoded splendour, its kitsch canvases and Napoleon III chandeliers, have been swallowed up inside the unattractive concrete tower blocks of the Marriott hotel where tourists no longer flock since 11 September. As for the ministry tower, it does not lack style: its summit is reminiscent of the Ancient Egyptian lotus flower, but this flower is square. Everything is modern, functional and efficient in this place where ambassadors and foreign dignitaries are greeted. In this contemporary arrangement, the minister's reception room and office stand out with elegant period furniture from the nineteenth century, reminding visitors that Egypt is a country with ancient and sophisticated diplomatic traditions.

In this period of crisis when all the landmarks seem to waver, Egyptian diplomacy is in the hands of Ahmed Maher, descended from a great family of pashas; his brother is greatly appreciated as ambassador to Paris, and their ancestor was King Farouk's prime minister. Beyond the vicissitudes, in the Nile Valley the state has a startling memory and permanence that are unparalleled in the region's other countries. And now state fragility, the ability or inability to endure after the torment that struck New York and Washington, is central to the chanceries' preoccupations. The minister chose the American University to hold a conference where he expressed his country's standpoint, while a press campaign across the Atlantic was showing indignation at the lukewarm tone of Egyptian support for the wounded US; such ingratitude was to be sanctioned through a drastic reduction of US aid for Egypt. We speak about this, that and everything else. At the Collège de la Sainte Famille in Faggala, the Mahers knew a Jesuit philosopher named Maurice Martin who, two decades later and with discreet confidence, would guide my first steps through the sociological labyrinth of the Nile Valley; he initiated so many of us, Muslims, Christians, Jews, believers, atheists, medievalists and anthropologists.

Tuesday 16 October

At the Faculty of Literature, Ain Shams University, Cairo. The name translates as 'sun spring' or 'eye of the sun'. I have always liked the beautiful, luminous name of this place where young people are initiated to knowledge. It could also signify 'sun spy', which has less charm, and evokes police surveillance and the reign of the secret service, a shadow – and how dark it was – in Nasser's rule. Throughout the region, the darkness has not dissipated entirely. Near the entrance gates, anti-riot police trucks are parked, and the students walk among them in the joyful, messy atmosphere of every university in the world.

Abu Skandar, who always drives by the university when he comes to Cairo from Heliopolis, has made this *passegiata* into his personal polling sample to measure the progress or regression of Islamic veiling. I secretly suspect him of privileging the qualitative aspect of the investigation over its strictly quantitative dimensions. In his defense, it is necessary to admit that one is easily perturbed by the appearance of female students in the Middle East. Cairo, Damascus, Beirut: the explosion of sensuality as one approaches campuses means that even veiling ends up inscribed on the level of the most disreputable fantasies, instead of erasing femininity from the landscape as its partisans wish. An entirely veiled silhouette opens only through a long slit where black eyes glitter; around her, colleagues shake out their wavy hair and move slowly, their feline walk emphasizing every curve of bodies outlined by very tight clothes. Veiled and 'naked' (according to the expressive terminology of the Islamist militants) merely highlight each other, bring each other out, serve as each other's foil in a perpetually moving game of one-upmanship.

During a lecture an Egyptian colleague and friend is giving, and in which I have been invited to take part, we discuss recent events. Only a little over a quarter of the class has seen the al-Jazeera airing of Osama Bin Laden's declaration on 7 October, in which he 'swears by God who raised the heavens without columns, that America will never sleep in peace as long as Israel oppresses Palestine'. The students here are from a relatively modest background, and probably do not have satellite antennas at home. A consensus takes shape to condemn terrorism that kills 'innocent civilians', in the words of a banner strung up in the quad: the victims of 11 September, but also Afghans under fire. Some mention that terrorism has claimed lives in Egypt in the past few years. One student explains that the whole affair is a conspiracy, that '4,500 influential Jews' (*kibar al-yahud*) received e-mail warnings on the night preceding the attacks not to go to their workplaces in the twin towers. While she elaborates on this ditty, which I have already heard ad nauseam since I arrived in the region, I notice Arabic grafitti scribbled on the door in chalk: 'There is no god but Allah/Israel is the enemy of Allah'. Another student, not veiled, was heretofore indifferent to Bin Laden, but fell under his charm when she saw and heard him on al-Jazeera. He alone, today, has redeemed the honour of Arabs and Muslims against America's arrogance and support for Sharon; he alone is concerned with the suffering of the Palestinians and Iraqis – even if he did not make much of it before. Nothing about the appearance of this young girl in jeans suggests sartorial adherence to the principles of extreme Islamist austerity that Bin Laden also incarnates. Thanks to his talents as a great communicator, he may well have succeeded in winning hearts far beyond the circles that share his sectarian ideology.

Someone tells me a *nukta*, one of those anecdotes everyone loves in the Middle East. Their load of humour, orally transmitted, serves as an antidote to the deadly official stereotypes. This one does not stand out for its sophistication: 'A woman heads towards the men's room in a restaurant. The staff try to stop her, and guide her towards the ladies'. She demands: "Is Osama Bin Laden in the restroom?" They reply in the negative. "So I can go in, because there is only one man left in the Arab and Muslim world: him".' Beyond its triviality, this story sums up quite well something I have noticed in conversation. 'Osama Bin Laden is the phallus!' one of the region's infrequent psychoanalysts tells me.

Wednesday 17 October
At Cairo Airport's police control, a functionary finds my passport, full of Arab visas, suspicious. He sends me off to have it checked in a room where it goes into a sort of infernal machine. It is flooded in white, red and blue rays of light, no doubt designed to reveal possible 'marks, corrections, deletions, alterations and additional remarks or pages', prohibited in the document under the heading 'important recommendations'. The policeman massaging it is a tall, fat, sweaty man, straddling a plastic chair that is too small for him. Another policeman is having an interminable conversation with his mother on a white telephone, placed on a little table where empty tea glasses pile up. During this scientific examination, I have time to observe the office. The ceiling is very high, as high as the airport hall itself. It has been decorated with an enormous

photograph, purchased where I do not know, and perhaps chosen for its gigantic size. The scene is New York at night, and in the middle, all lit up, are the twin towers of the World Trade Center.

Exonerated, I am allowed to return to the departure hall where my friend Gamal al-Ghitani is also waiting. He is going to France with a delegation of Egyptian writers and artists. We watch as four very athletic-looking young men with small rucksacks on their backs, one bearded, join the departing passengers. We half joke that they resemble the images of the 11 September hijackers, captured by security cameras in US airports: same demeanour. When the plane takes off, my neighbour, dreadfully distressed, begins to pray without leaving his seat; two or three other passengers follow suit. This is not the last of my surprises. We reach cruising altitude at the time of the noonday prayer, and the four young men, having performed their ablutions in the lavatory, unfold mats in front of the emergency exits and, turned towards Mecca, undertake the ritual prostrations and genuflections in the aisle. Gamal has never seen the likes of it on this airline, either. I remember Lubavitch Jews swaying and mumbling their prayers on a flight to New York, ten years ago, when I was going to see Rabbi Schneerson in Brooklyn to write a chapter about their movement for *The Revenge of God*. They were trying to convince all the 'ethnic' passengers (myself among them, despite my denials) to wear *tefillin*. Once they have completed their prayers, the four young men open their laptop and become absorbed in a video game.

Friday 19 October
On the Paris-Beirut flight, I bump into two Lebanese friends. This time I am in the front cabin, so there are few chances of seeing the aisle blocked by prayer mats. When I happen to fly in these conditions, on Middle Eastern or North African airlines, I always notice that almost everyone seems to know each other. The Arab universe of power, money and influence – a microcosm about as big as the aptly named 'club class' – is constantly criss-crossing the sky between its home base and Europe.

Last year on a flight to Algiers, I found myself seated near a man to whom person after person came to pay obeisance, remind him of a shared memory, bring so-and-so, who would call soon, to his attention, inquire with heartwarming solicitude about his health, be so bold as to mention the names of his children for whom prayers of success and happiness were pronounced, vouching for a relative. On arriving, I learned that my neighbour was the head of SONATRACH, the petrol company that accounts for almost 100 per cent of Algeria's export revenues.

Today I am travelling next to my 'colleague but friend nevertheless' – an expression of which he is fond – Ghassan Salameh. For a decade, we shared an office in Sciences Po, as well as many seminars, tutorials, dissertation committees; we relayed each other in finding resources and jobs for students, and built up an ironic complicity. He was appointed Minister of Culture and Francophonie in Lebanon a year ago, and I rarely ever see him anymore. We seized the opportunity to make this trip together in order to spend five hours in each other's company like old times, gossiping about colleagues, settling questions related to doctoral students and chatting about life.

The world summit on Francophonie should have been taking place in Beirut at around this time, and the new minister had worked around the clock to make it the success everyone was expecting. The 11 September attacks brought everything back to square one, and the summit has been postponed, *in sha' Allah*, until next year. On the other hand, the World Trade Organization, slightly more controversial after the protests in Seattle and Genoa, will take place in fifteen days in Qatar, a highly symbolic emirate: al-Jazeera's broadcasting centre, it is also within reach of Osama Bin Laden's missiles. Francophonie is more careful – or less enterprising – than trade. It is crushing that it has been unable to find the means of making itself heard just as the triumphant globalization and all-Americanization of the late twentieth century are being challenged by the yardstick of cultural pluralism, in the world we will be forced to build together.

Saturday 20 October

I am once more on my road to Damascus. In Beirut, during the civil war between 1975 and the end of the 1980s, *Tariq al-Sham* (as it is called) was the demarcation line from the port to the suburbs. To the east was the 'reactionary Christian' zone; to the west, the 'Islamo-progressives' – a spicy word combination, in retrospect. The war began clad in the ceremonial garb of the period's ideologies, bedecked with the local religious embroidery, and ended in the bloody tatters of bestial organized crime, where cynicism took doctrine's place and lucre stood in for any ideal. All this made a mockery of the grandiloquent proclamations in which each camp claimed to defend the sacred cause, according to the whim of constantly shifting alliances. In *His* name, children, women and the elderly were slaughtered pitilessly, just because they were in the wrong place at the wrong time – no matter if they had been born there. The massacre ended with accords signed in 1991 in Ta'ef, Saudi Arabia, under the aegis of the Wahhabi Sunni monarchy and while waiting for the promised manna of its petrodollars: they entrenched the Syrian protectorate over Lebanon and consecrated the supremacy of the prime minister – necessarily a Sunni Muslim – over the President of the Republic – necessarily a Maronite Christian.

Today, the city is a vast reconstruction site, under the auspices of businessman and Prime Minister Rafiq Hariri. The devastated downtown area has been rebuilt from scratch in the

Levantine-colonial style of the demolished buildings, and on weekends its trendy sidewalk cafés, reminiscent of Tel Aviv's to the iconoclastic wanderer, are packed. Sunnis or Maronites, winners and losers of the civil war, are demographically marginalized today by the Shi'ite community, which won the battle against Israel at the cost of bloody and unstoppable suicide attacks that forced the Hebrew State's army to evacuate South Lebanon. Before 11 September, the most powerful blows against the US or its allies in the Middle East came from the Shi'ite camp: the 1979 Iranian Revolution; the massacre of Marines and French soldiers from the multinational force in October 1983, which forced their armies to quit the country; and Israel's final retreat in 2000, seen as the first Arab military victory in living memory. The attacks on New York and Washington have changed the situation.

From time to time, carcasses of buildings gutted by bombs mark out the road.

Jacques Ferrandez has just sent me the album of Lebanese sketches he is publishing these days. We travelled this road together last year as far as the plains of the Beqaa. I recognize the houses he has pencilled or painted freehand with his little portable watercolour kit: a testament to the future, in the searing strokes of pencil or paintbrush, of Lebanon's atrocious wounds, of the suffering an abject, faceless war can cause – as America is discovering for the first time in the depths of its flesh.

At the Syrian-Lebanese border, I recognize the small customs house with its sweet red-tile roof in the style of the French Mandate after World War I. Two openings let cars through: private on one side, communal taxis on the other. I have not been down this road on the Syrian side in twenty-four years. When I was a fellow at the French Institute in Damascus, working myself to death to learn Arabic with no particular success under the authority of a Protestant director for whom such an apprenticeship could only be conceived of in suffering, my galley mates and I would flee the stifling atmosphere of a city where the dictatorship's weight could be felt even in interpersonal relations to spend a weekend in Beirut. Amidst the ruins of the unfortunately named 'Cannons' Square' (officially 'Martyrs' Square', which, alas, was equally appropriate), in the markets with bombed-out roofs, we found everything that was lacking in Syria's socialist penury – especially bread. I think that was the first concrete experience that allowed the left-wing student I was to touch the absurdity of a command economy. The main 'services', the communal taxis into which six of us would pile (antediluvian Mercedes that just wouldn't die or yellow Chevrolets) also picked up stocks of '*shami*' in Beirut: loaves of Oriental bread packaged in plastic. In Syria, the nationalized bakeries sold awful subsidized bread, hard and sometimes dangerous for teeth and stomachs: mixed in with the flour were substances like plaster and crushed pebbles; in it one might also discover ground glass and rusty staples. The station

One used to see nothing but portraits of Assad Sr. everywhere. They are still there – fewer of them, though, and many piously crossed out with a black band reminiscent of a cancelled postage stamp. In Morocco, I also noticed that the late Hasan II remains omnipresent in the iconography of power. The young King Muhammad VI, on the popular images one buys in Marrakesh's Jame' al-Fna' Square, straddles a jet-ski, swoops down the snowy slopes of Ifrane or undertakes the pilgrimage, clad in an *ihram*. But on official representations, he appears all the more sober and discreet because a portrait of his brother often accompanies him. The departed father, the two sons. Similarly, in Syria the brother's image completes the trinity – but this is a deceased brother; Basel, the elder, raised to rule, died when the Mercedes he was driving too fast crashed, a death in the manner of James Dean or Lady Di. He is often shown in combat trousers, eyes invisible behind dark Ray-Bans, a short fawn's beard framing his face, his figure muscular as though protecting his younger sibling, more frail in appearance and haunted by these two tutelary deaths.

It is said that this triptych projects the subliminal image of the Alawite holy trinity. The members of this religious minority have controlled power in Syria since 1963, and the Assad family emerged from it. The Alawites are said to venerate, on equal footing with the Prophet Muhammad, his son-in-law Ali and one of the first converts, Salman the Persian, which makes them execrable in the eyes of the most rigorous Sunnis – like Bin

Laden, say. However, he, too, is partial to representations of the trinity, where he is at the centre: in his carefully produced appearances on al-Jazeera, he is flanked by al-Zawahiri, the Egyptian doctor, and Abu Ghaith, the Kuwaiti football player. The subliminal message here harks back to the Prophet's epic: in his 'emigration' of 622, Muhammad fled idolatrous Mecca to take refuge in Medina. He returned, victorious, eight years later, expelling the infidels and declaring Islam. Osama Bin Laden sees himself in the 'remake' of this story for the age of satellite TV. Surrounded by his companions – like the *Sahaba*, the Prophet's venerated companions – in an arid landscape reminiscent of Arabia's desert, he fled Mecca, held by the 'hypocritical' Saud family, in a *hegira* of sorts to the Afghan mountains. He lets his supporters hope that he will return in the same manner, victorious, to the Holy City, to 'expel the Jews and Christians from the Arabian Peninsula'.

At the time, wars of religion were staked on raiding the rich caravans that transported myrrh, frankincense and slaves from Arabia Felix to Byzantium and Ctesiphon. Today, the raids target the oil and gas fields of Kuwait, Hasa and the coast of the Persian Gulf, which fuel most of the world's motors. The rest, the 'clash of civilizations', is all literature.

Syria, too, has become an oil producer. I did not remember that from quarter of a century ago, when I was a research fellow at the French Institute in Damascus, in the ochre stone house of the

Abu Rummaneh ('father pomegranate') quarter, on Shukri al-Assali ('honey-eyed Shukri') Street. In front of the window, I recognized the mulberry tree, its trunk thickened, and searched in vain for the cedar from which the Aleppine Marie Seurat picked enormous yellow fruits, once ripe, preparing exquisite preserves of which she sometimes gave me a spoonful for tea. Michel Seurat, a few years older than me, had already acquired a reputation as a rigorous and brilliant defender of the Arab cause, and was a scientific associate at the Institute. I admired him enormously. He was writing his dissertation under the supervision of Alain Touraine, read Arabic perfectly and effortlessly spoke the Damascus dialect. His wife was very beautiful, owned an Afghan hound and came to pick her husband up at the Institute in an old Alfa Romeo – which made the aforementioned Protestant director frown. Michel voted Communist.

Several times, they invited two or three young researchers over for dinner along with left-wing Syrian intellectuals to their Arab house behind the Hijaz train station, where a lemon tree grew in the kitchen. There were carpets, *mashrabiya*s and, once, even a pretty woman named Sheherazade, whom I eyeballed in silence and never saw again. I went to these evenings with pounding heart, very moved that I could tiptoe into a cenacle that so impressed me. It was also, one must confess, an opportunity to eat meat, because our stipends were so miserable, and paid so late, that we relied for nourishment mainly on *mana'ish*, those little star-shaped Damascene pastries smeared with oil and thyme.

One day in December 1977, having finally collected our small wages, we took off to Beirut without the director's knowledge, accompanied by Pierre-Jean Luizard, today our expert on Iraq. We dined in a real restaurant near the American University, where there were only a few customers. Those at the next table finished their meal, then emptied the till and held us up, relieving us of our meager fare. I remember the pistol, which my terror had made enormous, brandished before my eyes, and our attempts to explain that we agreed with the 'Islamo-progressive' camp (which controlled the territory we were on), before a slap closed our mouths.

And then that day in autumn of 1985, when I drove Michel Seurat to Orly airport to catch his flight to Beirut. Kidnapped when he landed, he was taken hostage by a faceless terrorist group – even then – that had styled itself 'Islamic Jihad'. He died in captivity, an atrocious death: isolated from his comrades, suffocated by coughing fits and – as Jean-Paul Kaufmann recounted – shouting: 'I'm not going to die here!' Jihad told the news agencies: 'We announce that the expert spy researcher has been executed …' I will never forget. My road to Damascus.

Sunday 21 October
Damascus's Christian neighbourhood, Qassaa, has preserved its spruce appearance. In September 1977, along with two other

research fellows – Lilly and Bertrand, cut down by AIDS like so many other Orientalist friends – I rented a small rooftop apartment. A penthouse, it was a makeshift lodging with very thin walls, which we had had to leave in a hurry with the first frost. Winters are cold in Damascus, and we used archaic stoves known as *sobia*, fired by intravenous doses of oil. We bought the oil from itinerant merchants who hauled tanks around on a donkey-drawn cart, their piercing cries – which we had fun imitating – ringing through the icy streets at dawn: 'Maaazouuut!' They mixed water in the petrol to increase profits: the flame would go out during combustion, then the oil would start to flow again, slowly inundating the floor and soaking it with its appalling odour. We would wake up in the morning, freezing cold, with headaches caused by the petrol fumes, and run a mop over the floor, late for class and cursing the vendors.

Today in Qassaa, I am going to see Michel Kilo, an opposition democrat who was imprisoned under the former regime, and whom Michel Seurat had defended in the international press, fearing for his life at one point. Michel Kilo has played an important role during this summer of 2001, creating 'discussion forums' that brought on a 'Damascus springtime'. Everyone has begun to speak, after decades of glacial silence. Many hoped that the young president, whose close aides were giving discreet signs of encouragement, would lead a transition to democracy by making representatives of the middle classes partners in power. Very quickly, the forums began to criticize the old regime, and his tutelary barons reminded Bashar al-Assad whose son he was. The discussion circles closed down, one after another. Still, as in the old popular democracies of Eastern Europe where the secret services oversaw the quiet fall of communism, part of the Syrian intelligence apparatus is attempting to prevent the system's collapse, and to co-opt the most digestible elements of the educated young generation into the arcana of power.

I will meet two Alawite dignitaries of the regime during the day. I am struck by the shared physical characteristics: heavy-set, with the long cranium and flat occiput of Hafez al-Assad's ubiquitous portraits – as if they were all from the same ethnic group somewhere in central Asia, perpetuated by consanguinous marriages. High society in Damascus and Aleppo looked on in horror as these despised peasants' sons reached power, owing their sudden promotion to having signed up in the French army during the Levant Mandate. It snickered, attributing the flat-backed skull to a slap behind the ears, administered in their mountain village as they were told: '*Yallah! Ruh al-Sham!*' – 'Go on! March on Damascus!'

Those I am speaking to have PhDs and enjoy contact with intellectuals and academics, Syrians and foreigners alike. The first has a very large office, lined with books carefully organized on glass-fronted shelves. On the side walls, two immense colour photographs of President Bashar and his late brother Basel face each other in full length, floor to ceiling. They remind me of the colossal faces of the kings of Commagene, carved into the rock of the Turkish plateau. In the other office the hall is adorned with an almost primitive painting of Hafez al-Assad on a white horse, banner in hand, painted after the Iranian Shi'ite portraits of Ali, the Prophet's son-in-law. I am told that Syria has suffered from terrorism (meaning the attacks carried out by the Muslim Brothers), which was particularly relentless in hounding the 'brothers from the coast' (meaning the Alawites, originally from the coastal mountains). I hear that the problem would have been settled promptly if only the West – the same West that today seeks to bring all the Middle Eastern states on board in a war against terrorism – had not put up obstacles to the vigorous elimination of the troublemakers, in the name of respect for human rights; that all efforts will be fruitless if the causes of anti-Western sentiment are not dealt with by settling the Palestinian problem, for a thousand Bin Ladens will arise to replace this one; that no one understands why Europe does not have a policy independent of America's; that one must be suspicious of the clerics' doublespeak, for while today they may preach calm to the masses, tomorrow they will be the first to whip them into a frenzy if they feel the wind turn.

Tuesday 23 October
The Résidence des Pins, where the French ambassador to Beirut lives, was unlucky enough, during the Lebanese civil war, to

find itself on the front line between the 'Christian' east and the 'Islamo-progressive' west. It was devastated, bombed by all the militias, and all that remains of the forest that gave it its name is a scanty cluster of slender sea pines, miraculously spared by bombs and fire. Their tall silhouettes, lonely and distinguished, testify to the Levant's glorious past, now gone. In the adjoining hippodrome, a few children from good families exercise their horses, which snort in the early morning smell of fresh manure. Ficus trees, indifferent to the wounds inflicted by men's murderous fury, have sprouted disorderly new branches over those that had been broken, in a commingling of green leaves. The trees have thickset, sturdy white trunks through which the lively, powerful sap flows. The most rustic species survived the battles, taking the place of the elegant, fragile strains.

In this residence, restored today in very confident taste, I am awoken at dawn by martial accents borne by a metallic-sounding loudspeaker. Darting an eye over the balcony, I glimpse the courtyard invaded by parachutists in combat gear, clutching machine-guns. For an instant, I imagine that war has come prowling back this way to claim new victims, that some unknown twist in the hunt for Bin Laden has occurred during the night. Yet the soldiers seem debonair. They are French, pose for photographs on the porch, then carry out their manoeuvres under the orders of an NCO who straightens the ranks and leads the march, counting out '*wan – too! wan – too!*' in a way that reminds me of the actor who played Adjutant Daube in *The*

Good Soldier Švejk, a play my father adapted in the 1960s from the novel of Jaroslav Hašek, and his '*Hup – too! hup – too!*'. They wear the sky-blue beret and scarf of the United Nations forces: UNIFIL soldiers from south Lebanon, on the border with Israel, come to pay homage to their 56 comrades killed exactly eighteen years ago in the attack on the Drakkar building – at the same time as 241 Marines. France and the US, knocked out by the first terrorist attack on such a scale against the West, pulled out the soldiers of the Multinational Force they had sent to Beirut to separate the combatants after Christian militias massacred Palestinians in the camps at Sabra and Shatila, under the indifferent gaze of Israeli troops stationed a few hundred metres away. The Multinational Force packed its flags and left Lebanon, abandoning it to Syrian tutelage.

The ceremony unfolds in front of the residence's monument to the dead. We are lined up in two columns, facing each other, military men on one side, civilians on the other. The ambassador, Philippe Lecourtier, lays a wreath on the monument. The colonel reads out the victims' names and ranks, one after another, and after each name a captain with a Spanish surname shouts out, emphasizing the first and last word: 'Dead for France!' The civilians are facing east and the sun is blinding us, stinging our eyes. We put on dark glasses. I hear someone mention 'Lieutenant Dejean de la Bâtie'. My children have friends from school called Dejean de la Bâtie. This little detachment of soldiers, the handful of civilians in the residence's big park, the cluster of forsaken pines in the metallic clarity of this Levantine autumn morning, in this, the first year of the new millennium, a month and a half after the attacks on New York and Washington. On a marble plaque by the monument to the military dead, on the list of civilian victims, Michel Seurat's name is engraved.

The quarter of Haret Hreik, in the southern suburbs, was once a Christian village. A church remains, surrounded by a high fence to ward off pillaging. The fountain wears the insignia of the Islamic Republic of Iran, and also a stencilled design representing Hizbullah's logo – the first *l* of 'Allah', in the Arabic calligraphy, extended into an arm brandishing a machine gun. There are only Shi'ites left in the neighbourhood: the Christians have fled.

I had come here last year for the first time. On every lamp-post, the 'Party of God' had hung hyperrealist, hypnotic portraits of 'martyrs' – all the same type, like blown-up ID pictures, the men wearing the same combat gear, short beards and clouded eyes. Only the names and faces were different. Today, the images of these dead have disappeared. I had thought I would enter a bit of Tehran, with women forced to veil under the punctilious control of pious militias and other vice squads made up of young lumpenproletarians. This is not the case. Women generally walk about bareheaded. Quite a few ladies have the bleached blond hair that Lebanese fashionistas so adore. Hizbullah has gone bourgeois. The former terrorist group, manipulated by the Islamic Republic of Iran, which advocated 'Islamic revolution in Lebanon' and was very involved in taking Westerners hostage in the 1980s, later became the 'Islamic resistance' party. It expelled the Israelis and their mercenaries, the 'South Lebanon Army', freeing the country and acquiring a Lebanese nationalist aura even among Maronite Christians. Today, through its charity networks – institutions it founded – it is allowing Shi'ite rural migrants to make their ascent in the urban and political world, a little like the French Communist Party and workers' unions turned Italian or Polish proletarians, who had immigrated to Lorraine or the north during the first half of the twentieth century, into French petits-bourgeois.

In Islamist bookshops, I purchase photos of Sheikh Nasrallah, the head of Hizbullah, holding up a machine-gun taken from Israeli troops, in a montage that depicts him standing before the Dome of the Rock in Jerusalem, the target of the future reconquest – an ideal warrior, intended to galvanize the masses. Is he more real than the dream of proletarian dictatorship that the Communist Party fed its militants as it became involved in the daily management of working-class municipalities, where its revolutionary fibre would wear thin? I do not know. There are many French translations of Islamist literature in these bookshops, even children's books. This propaganda in Molière's tongue is destined for the Lebanese of

West Africa, most of them Shi'ites, who have controlled trade there since they fled to the jungle, away from the misery of the arid mountains, at the time when Lebanon, like Senegal or Guinea, had fallen under the shared tutelage of the French colonial empire. Most have forgotten Arabic, but preserved an attachment to country and religion that translates into generous gifts. These may allow the more certain purchase of places in paradise that fortunes accumulated in Africa, under sometimes controversial conditions, might not have guaranteed. The huge buildings dripping with marble, housing charity foundations and hospitals destined for the community, testify to this particular generosity and to the financial links between the diaspora and the Party of God.

I have an appointment with Sayyid Muhammad Hussein Fadlallah – the title *sayyid* signifies that he claims direct descent from the Prophet's family, while his family name translates as 'God's favour'. He has long been considered as Hizbullah's mentor, its spiritual guide. Marie Seurat had met with him when Michel was being held hostage somewhere in the southern suburbs, to try and get her husband freed – unsuccessfully. Since then, he has moved away from politics and the party, cultivating the role of 'doctor of law' that his great religious erudition affords him. His disciples consider him a *marja'* – a supreme authority, a source of emulation which confers upon him, among those Shi'ites who revere him, a sort of infallibility comparable to that which the Pope enjoys in the eyes of the most fervent Catholics. He expresses himself in the limpid Arabic of the great religious orators, tinged with a slight Iraqi accent – the accent of the country where he was born and educated, in Shi'ite sanctuaries, until the age of eighteen. As when I visited Arafat, I have to leave my cell phone with security – everyone remembers the phone, booby-trapped by the Israeli secret service, that killed 'Engineer Ayyash', Palestinian Hamas's bomb expert.

A disciple records our conversation; although he does not speak French, he wants to know if he can take a correspondence course at Sciences Po in Paris. Sayyid Fadlallah does not give Bin Laden much credit: he sees him as one of those 'temporary saviours' (*munqidh al-zaman*) who appeal to the sentimentalism of the region's peoples – like Nasser, Khomeini and Saddam Hussein. He does not see him lasting long, given his lack of 'capacities' (*imkaniyyat*). He must not be able to muster much esteem for a Bin Laden whose extremely austere Sunnism, borne of the Wahhabi doctrine prevailing in Saudi Arabia, has always horrified Shi'ites – as a pamphlet (in French) titled *The Wahhabi Heresy*, which I have just purchased at the bookshop on the corner, reminds me. I am more taken aback to hear Khomeini placed in the same category as the others. From the height of his religious prestige, is the Sayyid bringing the ayatollah down to the level of politicians – especially since he makes no effort to hide his fundamental disagreements with Khomeini's successor and the Islamic Republic of Iran's current guide, Khamenei? Or is he implying that the time of the Islamic revolution, and the chimeras it engendered, is past?

Wednesday 24 October

I am waiting for a young colleague at the main entrance to the American University in Beirut, on Bliss Street, Ras Beirut – the city's peak. This neighbourhood used to be called 'the Republic of Ras Beirut', a sort of Arab hybrid between Saint-Germain-des-Près in the 1960s and the republic of letters; a bit of Lebanon where all the intellectuals banned by the region's many dictators sought refuge and remade the world, communing in a nationalism tinged with anti-imperialism and socialism, before the civil war blew down this 'dream palace of the Arabs'. Many of these ideas, which seemed so seductive in the quarter's smoky cafés, amidst the bookshops where one could find every book and newspaper from all over the world, censored by the despots in neighbouring countries, fed the war's destructive folly. The intellectuals went back into the protective cocoons of each community, and those who had tasted Sartre, Berque or Frantz Fanon together ended up disemboweling each other, reduced to their primitive identities: Christian and Muslim, Maronite, Greek Orthodox, Druze, Sunni and Shi'ite.

Today, in the place of these cafés and bookshops, a glittering McDonald's has just opened, its neon lights ablaze, demonstrating the equalizing power of the hamburger on the students who, cell phones glued to their ears, are taking a break

between classes. How many have downloaded the latest logo –
a close-up of Bin Laden, taken from an image broadcast on al-
Jazeera, and, in the background, the plane crashing into the
twin towers? A little later a colleague from Tripoli, a sizeable
city with a Sunni majority in the north of the country, will tell
me that the most popular name in the maternity wards of his
town since 11 September is none other than Osama.

Friday 9 November
The flight to Dubai is packed. Despite the airlines' complaints,
the social plans they have launched and the subsidies they have
received, since the events in New York and Washington I have
travelled on planes that have almost all been full. There is an
infinite diversity of languages and races in the cabin: Europeans,
Americans, Africans, Asians, Arabs – an accurate reflection of
the population in this emirate, where 95 per cent of the
inhabitants are foreigners. For once, I recognize no one in the
cosmopolitan, anonymous crowd. No such luck, however. My
neighbour is a young Arab girl who quickly takes off her jacket,
for it is too warm. Her bare arms, the French newspapers she is
reading: all the signs indicate that she is a North African from
France. Yet her hair, her choice of clothes and trainers, do not fit
any known variation on *Beur* girls' style. A glance tells me she
has also noticed something not quite right about me, an odd
European who is reading, in Arabic, the transcript of Sheikh
Yusuf al-Qaradawi's religious programme, broadcast the

previous week on al-Jazeera and printed from the *jazeera.net* website. She must have wondered if I was Lebanese, then been dissatisfied with this hypothesis. The distribution of the menu, the delicate matter of choosing between 'French regional cuisine' and 'Chinese flavours' (which the flight attendant renders prosaically as 'chicken or fish?'), provide us with the pretext for conversation. Her name, Khulud, means 'eternity'. She is Egyptian, went to a French secondary school, and we discover that we know many of the same people in Cairo. She is from a good family; some of her cousins are Muslim Brothers. She has just seen her sister, whose demeanour is as liberated as hers, on the BBC, declaring her sympathy for Bin Laden, who has withstood the US. Khulud recently married and settled in London, although she speaks English poorly. She had the opportunity to live in Paris, but did not take it, she explains: a young Frenchman, converted to Islam in Egypt – who, I am stunned to discover, attended my classes long ago – asked for her hand in marriage. But he insisted that she wear the veil in order for him to take her to France. She burst out laughing as she refused this unprecedented condition for the acquisition of a French passport.

At the front desk of the hotel where I am staying in Dubai, a mustachioed Indian with the dark skin of a Tamil is enthroned. Behind him, five clocks show local time and the time in New York, London, Moscow and Baku respectively. The 'reception' sign is written in English and Russian. There are also five discotheques with poetic and evocative names: Caspian Nightclub, Madness Club, Cohiba Bar ... In the foyer, the picture of an 'artistic troupe from Russia' appearing in one of the clubs takes as its pretext the acrobatics of the Kazachok to show three blonde girls in white shorts, naked thighs spread wide. Floods of metallic music escape when a door opens to let a client pass through. Each club has an ethnic speciality. At the Cohiba, the hostesses are Slavic; elsewhere, Uzbek, Caucasian, Filipina or Bengali. A reddish light bathes the atmosphere, striated by white spotlights that sweep across the floor, where the girls are dancing alone. The stale odour of alcohol seems to impregnate the walls, the rancid scent of beer mingling with whisky's acrid vapours. In the clouds of cigarette smoke, Arabs from the peninsula are seated before their glasses, clad in *dishdash*es, the long white robes that are their traditional costume. Headdresses – the way of wearing a turban or a *kuffiyeh* – make it possible to tell apart Saudis, Omanis, residents of the Emirates, Bahrainis or Qataris, with whom Levantines and Egyptians in European clothes mingle. Dubai by night.

Saturday 10 November
Fly and Buy. Dubai. The emirate is the entire region's emporium, seizing the crown from Lebanon, which once played the same role. The civil war brought precipitous ruin to 'the

Middle East's Switzerland', and Dubai took its place. Some Lebanese today dream of yesterday's deals returning. They hope the US's liquidation of the Taliban and the region-wide crisis will turn trade flows away from the emirate and bring them back towards Beirut. As evidence, they cite the large number of buildings that sprout from the ground and remain quietly empty, their façades inscribed with the words TO LET and a telephone number in giant characters. But Dubai apparently has a thousand other resources, and Beirut's aces seem paltry by comparison. The emirate has managed to become an extraordinary depot-city, which could claim descent from fifteenth-century Venice or Amsterdam. It irrigates a vast region, which largely transcends the Middle East in the narrow sense to stretch from the former Soviet empire to the Maghreb and India, with rapidly accessible products at the most competitive prices, while providing its extremely wealthy petrol neighbours from the Peninsula with the luxury goods they adore. Cars and perfumes, aluminium and gas, gold and computer technology: Dubai excels in every branch of global commerce, along a spectrum that embraces the archaic and the post-modern, from precious metals to e-business.

Of the ancient trade through the Persian Gulf, there remain, on the quay, the famous dhows of Pirate Coast – as the English named the region (gratuitously, and better to justify its conquest, insists an historical work published by the emir of Sharjah). Today, for the most part, the sailboats take on Iranian and Pakistani crews. The men cram mountains of cartons full of second-rate goods into the hold and on deck, where they will cook in the sun and imbibe the sea spray during the Gulf crossing: old air-conditioning units, used household appliances, dented cars – everything that gets thrown away here, where wealth is brand new, and recycled in the poor countries on the other side. Sometimes, I am told, Baluchi or Iranian pirates take the boats by surprise, immediately throw the sailors – whose families are too poor to pay ransom – overboard to the sharks, and pillage the cargo of bits and pieces, placing their victims' lives lower than even this miserable booty. But these relics of the past count for little in the emirate's prosperity. Coastal navigation has given way to large-scale international trade. Russian, Bulgarian, Ukrainian, Pakistani, Indian or Algerian airplanes relay each other constantly to carry away the unbeatably-priced merchandise that huge cargo ships unload, anchored in deep water at the port. Last year at Oran Airport, I remember having seen advertisements for 'fly and buy' trips to Dubai, which have all but replaced the suitcase trade in which the *trabendistes*, Algiers's small-time smugglers, customarily indulged first with Marseilles, then Barcelona. And in Kabul, in 1998, I noticed that the Taliban's 4x4s, equipped with machine-guns on the back – the better to enjoin good and prohibit evil – boasted, side by side with pious bumper stickers, license plates from Dubai or a neighbouring emirate.

Life seems good – as long as one is a rentier-citizen or a white expatriate, maybe even an Indian with highly valued skills in accounting or computer technology. Excellent restaurants, fine French wines, trendy California-style cafés, no entry visas for Europeans, wide highways lit up as bright as day all night, for big-engined air-conditioned cars with impeccably shiny body work, a skyline that would like to compete with that of an American city and even ... a 'World Trade Center'. Amateurs of civilizational authenticity, move right along. In response to those who take offense at the artificial veneer of modern urbanism applied to a world of Bedouins and pearl divers and who doubt that these mushroom-cities, where wealth is concentrated in the hands of a tiny minority of citizens, can survive for long, British anthropologist Paul Dresch has noted that the same could be said of the glorious ancient cities of Palmyra or Petra. Springing up in a few years around a sudden flow of commercial prosperity, they borrowed construction materials from Athens or Rome, copied their urban planning regulations, reproduced cardo, decumanus, forum and draughtboard pattern, were populated by a majority of metics and slaves deprived of civic rights, and prospered for long centuries.

From time to time one meets vehicles that look like livestock trucks, loaded with the closest thing to modern slaves: Pakistani construction workers. Teams work in shifts around the clock; enormous projectors light up the sites. They have neither the right to strike nor social security, and know that any act of disobedience will be punished by immediate expulsion. These people are at the very bottom of the ladder. They might make 300 euros a month, of which they send half back home. With the remainder, they pay rent on their dormitories and buy basic foodstuffs: rice, oil, sugar, tea. In Pakistan, they would be jobless, perhaps recruited by the *ulema* of the popular *madrasa*s to swell the ranks of demonstrators brandishing Bin Laden's portrait in front of television cameras desperate for sensational images. Waiting to cross the Afghan border, afflicted by the gnawing of boredom and fleas in Peshawar's hotel rooms, cameramen have smothered viewers with close-ups of Uncle Sam in effigy, burning as children brandish plastic Kalashnikovs and a mullah, thrilled to be on TV, chants rhythmic *Allahu Akbar*s. The beards, too, want their fifteen minutes of fame – Andy Warhol's vision of modern man's ultimate ambition.

Sharjah, the emirate that neighbours Dubai, serves as its dormitory town. Rents there are lower. The local potentate, fond of culture, has had a museum built and a traditional, fake but quite charming quarter reconstituted near the port. He is also more of a stickler for public morality and Islamic norms.

Sharjah University could be a mirage straight out of an historical Hollywood blockbuster. Around an immense avenue planted with palm trees, the proportions of which evoke the Mall in Washington, stand neo-classical buildings like the edifices L'Enfant dreamed up to house Congress, the White House, etc. But these have the Herculean proportions afforded by the desert's infinite space and petrol's extravagant abundance. The avenue marks off girls' and boys' faculties. Every field of study is divided in two, to avoid the poisonous temptations of integration. But in this field, human creativity is unbounded, and so big signs in Arabic and English make it clear that campus parking lots are off limits to cars with tinted windows ... Petroleum rents make it imperative for any self-respecting student to arrive at university at the wheel of an enormous Land Cruiser, customized as a private dwelling with a bar (alcohol or Coca-Cola) and music (techno or Islamist sermons), far from the moral constraints and proprieties of the family abode. In the parking lot, one can pick out the cars belonging to professors (most of them foreigners), far smaller than the students'. The American University building closes off the perspective of this immense sand mall. There, classes are taught in English, and boys and girls mingle on the benches – as if the language of Shakespeare, McDonald's and Microsoft could mithridatize students against the dangers of co-education.

National origins are more diverse, too. The class where I am lecturing is a microcosm of the Islamic *ummah*: a veiled Iraqi sits next to a Kuwaiti boy in jeans; a Wahhabi Saudi in *dishdash* and chequered *kuffiyeh* rubs elbows with Shi'ite Iranians, Pakistanis, Emiratis and Omanis. Palestinians, Syrians,

Lebanese and Egyptians make up the bulk of the contingent. Here, in contrast to Ain Shams University in Cairo, all the students saw Bin Laden's announcement, broadcast by al-Jazeera on 7 October. Satellite television is one of the bare necessities for these American-accented offspring of wealthy families. As elsewhere, the girls are the ones who show the most enthusiasm for Osama. The young Iraqi and her Palestinian classmates commune in praise, describing their emotion when they heard Bin Laden swear by God, who raised the skies without pillars, that America would never enjoy security as long as Israeli tanks were crushing Palestine, and Iraq was afflicted by the embargo. 'He stood up to defend us. He is the only one.' Their Kuwaiti neighbour doesn't say a word. The *dishdash*-clad Saudi student introduces a nuance: 'Bin Laden is a billionaire. Why didn't he bother about Palestine immediately after the end of the Afghan *jihad*? It's too easy to raise these issues now, to widen his support base when he is under attack …' What do they think of his most recent declarations, his diatribes against the West as a whole, the United Nations and Kofi Annan? Most have not seen them on television. Some have heard about them, and consider that he has made a political mistake. But everyone is vehemently opposed to American policy, the attack on Afghanistan, the bombing of 'innocent civilians'. (The debate is conducted in good English, which would certainly allow them to find jobs in the United States). I am asked to explain, to define France's position. They are very pleasant and courteous, but where the crowds of lefties, eco-warriors and other Third-Worldists will not penetrate. A visa is necessary to enter Qatar, and is only granted if one has a guarantor – or a sponsor – on-site. The country has attained universal notoriety since the Arabic-language satellite channel al-Jazeera – which is to the war of Autumn 2001 what CNN was to the Gulf War in 1991 – set up business here. People know about Qatar thanks to al-Jazeera – just as some Japanese or Australian tourists may have discovered France's existence because Paris is only half an hour away from EuroDisney. It is therefore in the land of al-Jazeera, a channel the US administration regularly incriminates for its broadcasts of Bin Laden's incendiary proclamations, that the World Trade Organization, a body devoted to encouraging free economic exchange for the profit of American imperialism – according to José Bové and other opponents of globalization – is meeting.

The Qatari state, which demonstrated its acute understanding of global power relations to the extent of creating al-Jazeera, could not let itself be overtaken by novices in media manipulation: our Roquefort-sandwichman, Great Destroyer of McDonald's, has obtained a visa. The scene is well set for the photo ops: José Bové, mouth sealed by masking tape stuck beneath his large mustache, useless pipe in hand, closely watched by security guards in *dishdash* and *kuffiyeh*. A snapshot in the next day's international press, and the WTO meeting took place quietly, with a celebration of human rights-era China's entry to the global business club, *al-hamdulillah*! The delegates have few distractions in the emirate: lacking Seattle's demos and rioters, they get their thrills by visiting the locals at the scandalous al-Jazeera headquarters – where English- or French-speaking journalists are mobilized to welcome and guide whole groups of these pilgrims to the sacred sanctuary of Arab television's Mecca. Global commerce is paying homage to the merchandizing of Bin Laden products – the man himself is apparently hidden in the Pashtun mountains, a missile strike away from the Qatari peninsula. We must be on the front line of the famous 'clash of civilizations' – but I am no longer sure which side we are on.

I had visited the channel's headquarters in 1997, and been impressed by the journalists' professionalism and the state-of-the-art equipment, which many European television channels might have envied. But today is not the day for reunions, in the midst of this crowd of voyeurs. Nor do I have anything to do in the big hotels where the WTO sessions are taking place. I have come to Qatar to take advantage of the presence of Sheikh Yusuf al-Qaradawi, who is at al-Jazeera shooting his Sunday program, which is broadcast live: *al-Shari'a wal-Hayat* ('Islamic Law and Life'). It sets the tone for Arabic-language Sunni sermons across the world. For the past twenty-odd years, I have been observing the career, statements and travels of this former Muslim Brother, jailed under Nasser, who then left

Egypt for Qatar, receiving that country's nationality (a rare distinction). The mentor of Islamist students in Sadat's Egypt, where I saw him haranguing crowds gathered for Eid prayers, he was brought in to help Algerian President Chadhli confer a measure of religious legitimacy on the FLN regime in the years preceding the birth of the FIS. He is the spiritual guide of young Islamist militants in Western Europe; a prolific author, translated into several languages – for a time, the French minister of the interior prohibited the sale in France of his book, *The Licit and the Illicit in Islam*; the on-line host of the Yusuf al-Qaradawi homepage on the Net; and a member of the *Shari'a* board of the biggest Islamic banks (the *Shari'a* board is their religious monitoring council, responsible for ensuring that financial transactions conform to the injunctions of the sacred texts; the *ulema* who belong to such boards have to be of superior standing to pull clients). In other words, Yusuf al-Qaradawi is (almost) everywhere one finds Sunni Islam. And his Sunday programme on al-Jazeera is the cornerstone of this edifice; it has come to confer upon this 'practicing cathodic' a notoriety that allows him to surpass all his peers. Jealousy has not been absent in a world where religious hierarchies are fluid – in contrast to Catholicism. A visible *ulema* must fight constantly for his market shares against rivals who, in their bid to destroy him, will have recourse to states or financial pressure groups interested in promoting their causes. A few days before our meeting, al-Qaradawi was barred from entry at the border which Islamic law's passion for codification (like that of Judaism) does not take offense. *The Licit and the Illicit in Islam* is full of codifications of sexuality and positions for intercourse. Nor did Sheikh al-Qaradawi hesitate to make headlines by declaring on television – in response to a specific question – that cunnilingus and fellatio were licit. He takes up the entire spectrum of televised material, from the sermon to the talk show. He has an answer to everything – and a planet-wide audience thinks that Islam speaks through him. This is why I am curious to hear his precise position on Bin Laden, the 11 September attacks, the war in Afghanistan and the immediate fate of the Muslim world. His opinion is a fairly good harbinger of conservative religious sentiment, of the pious middle classes and other bourgeois Islamists whose support is crucial to the success of any revolutionary enterprise undertaken in the name of religion. Conversely, when the militant radicals frighten these groups, the former, deprived of financial and social relays and support, have no chance of transforming their 'clashes in the pan' or terrorist operations into lasting mobilization and of seizing the power they crave. Sheikh al-Qaradawi is a cold-blooded *ulema*, grounded in the body of his dogmatic knowledge, impassive to the passing crazes of the sentimental masses, the digressions of the 'Arab street', the agitation of journalists and students hanging on Osama's words and attire at the mouth of his cave.

An appointment is set at Qatar University – where he is head of a religious studies department. The setting is appropriate for a meeting between professors, a 'crusading' French Orientalist on one hand, a 'fundamentalist' *ulema* attached to his doctor's title on the other. Beyond the mutual prejudices, the lack of illusions each of us nurtures with regard to the other, something will come to pass in this discussion between professionals – or so I hope. I am surprised by the premises, located behind a parking lot, at the end of the university grounds in an encampment surrounded by sand far from the luxury of the other buildings, which are drowning in verdant vegetation irrigated by petro-money. Everyone knows that the sheikh is not exactly poor: the modesty of the place where he receives visitors expresses detachment from material things, which university learning is supposed to stimulate.

He receives me punctually and cordially. He expresses himself in the Arabic of the *ulema*, fluid and solidly constructed, which seems to flow naturally; when the conversation grows more relaxed, he passes into Egyptian dialect, which creates a feeling of proximity between us, despite the age difference (he was born in 1926). He is not wearing either the caftan I had always seen him in, nor is his head capped as usual with the red fez encircled with a white turban – the outfit of al-Azhar's laureates. He wears everyday clothes, Qatari-style: a white *dishdash*, and on his head a sort of white veil, which he adjusts periodically. Dressed like that, he reminds me of certain Moroccan rabbis I had interviewed in 1990 in the working-class cities of southern Israel for my book, *The Revenge of God*.

Behind his desk, a large glass-fronted bookcase holds collections of works in Muslim theology – a fairly diversified corpus, which is not limited to the Wahhabi vulgate distributed throughout the world by Saudi associations. Everywhere on his desk are bundles of paper covered in delicate, well-formed calligraphy – he remains a man of the pen, and no doubt others are responsible for managing his website. We mention a conference where we had argued in Paris, in 1994, under the auspices of the Union of Islamic Organizations in France. (I had been very violently taken to task by an Algerian Islamist militant who had long been loitering in France and was in cahoots with a French politician; he hated the book I had just published on the implantation of these same movements in the West, *Allah in the West*.)

When I ask him what he thinks of Bin Laden, whether he considers his declarations important from a religious viewpoint, I am told that the person in question has never published anything that would allow one to judge his learning on actual evidence; he could not possibly call himself a doctor in law, and therefore can pass no juridical opinion, or *fatwa*: he is a 'preacher' (*wa`iz*) – the lowest rank in the current hierarchical classification. It is this absence of knowledge that caused him to commit the fundamental mistake of launching a *jihad* against the West: for al-Qaradawi, this no longer has any meaning today, where the Internet and satellite television are available. The propagation and expansion of Islam, proselytism, can take place through these media, without violence. The *jihad* against the West could undermine years of patient implanting, and spread suspicion.

The sheikh fulminates against Bin Laden's spokesman, the Kuwaiti football player Abu Ghaith (ironically dubbed 'Bin Ghaith'), who has called on Muslims to stop taking airliners in anticipation of a forthcoming attack, and encouraged his co-religionists dwelling in the West to return. For these reasons, and to avoid the perception of America's Muslims as a fifth column, al-Qaradawi has signed a *fatwa* taken by an American *ulema* of Egyptian origin, who authorized Muslim soldiers in the US army to go and fight the Taliban. This has caused a commotion: on 20 October, in Damascus, I watched Muslims in the US debate the topic on al-Jazeera; the *ulema* in question was on the set – a fat man who spoke Arabic with a whining American accent unlikely to win him the sympathies of Middle Eastern women viewers fascinated by Bin Laden. The regional press attacked him sharply; but Sheikh al-Qaradawi's support has perturbed a few of his detractors.

I muse aloud: if it is licit for Muslim American soldiers to fight the Taliban, can the Taliban's war against the US, which is bombing their territory, be considered a *jihad* anyway? For al-Qaradawi, there is no question about it: this is precisely the case of 'defensive *jihad*' provided for in the sacred texts. The American bombs mean that non-Muslim armies are attacking Islamic territory: Mullah Omar has good reason to call for the general mobilization of his co-religionists all over the planet. I take the line of questioning further: when the Taliban defend themselves against the assaults of the Northern Alliance – made up of Muslim combatants – do they have the right to declare *jihad* and call on believers for assistance? The answer falls like a guillotine: No – this is not a *jihad*, in any way.

The cause of Bin Laden and the Taliban now seems to me to be in serious jeopardy. The *ulema* will not mobilize in their support, beyond a superficial solidarity with Afghanistan, which will cease as soon as the Alliance's combatants have upended the balance of power on the ground. They already took Mazar-i Sharif yesterday, and it matters little that the Uzbek general Rashid Dostom, who occupied the city, has never been a paragon of piety – since the time when he served the pro-Soviet communist regime in Kabul. In the *ulema*'s eyes, as long as it is possible to present him as a 'sociological' Muslim, any declaration of *jihad* against him is invalid.

Is any defensive *jihad* valid in today's world? The sheikh cites Kashmir (against the Indians), Chechnya (against the Russians) and especially Israel. Are the suicide attacks committed by the Islamist party Hamas and others licit? The response is affirmative. Yet he had previously explained to me that he condemned outright the massacre of innocent civilians in the 11 September attacks. What about when a bomb explodes in a Tel Aviv pizza parlour and kills the civilians present? Answer: Israel is a military society, men and women serve in the army, therefore there can be no innocent civilians. All are legitimate targets for *jihad*.

One of the sheikh's other appointments enters the room and joins us – according to the Oriental custom that keeps no one waiting in the antechamber but allows audiences to overlap, as they arrive at the *diwan*. During the greetings, I lose my line of questioning. I was thinking about texts from *al-Ansar*, published by the GIA – Algeria's Armed Islamic Group – justifying the assassination of civilians and even of children in the cafés of Algiers during the civil war in the 1990s, and I wanted to know whether and how the sheikh (who devoted a widely viewed programme to that war in 1996) reacted to the massacre of children – Israeli children in this case. For there is little doubt that, once fantasies of Bin Laden's triumph have evaporated, the Arab-Israeli conflict will become the focal point for grievances once again, reinforced by the frustration of all those who praised him to the skies. But the arrival of a new guest presses the encounter towards its conclusion, and I submit a final question: at the end, after this *jihad* hastily triggered by Bin Laden turns against its authors, does the Muslim world not run the risk of sinking into a new *fitna*, the internal sedition, chaos and anarchy against which the *ulema* have always warned, wielding the double-edged sword of *jihad* parsimoniously for this purpose throughout the fourteen centuries of Muslim history? The answer comes in Egyptian dialect: today, we are experiencing not one *fitna* but two (*mish fitna bas fitnatayn*). The first was that of Saddam Hussein in 1990: the universe of Islam emerged from it broken for the long term; the second, that of 11 September 2001, will only deepen the breaches and extend the fault lines that divide the community of believers, while reinforcing their enemies' power.

Monday 12 November

The emirate of Abu Dhabi is the wealthiest of the United Arab Emirates, thanks to its petroleum resources. Sheikh Zayed, who has overseen its destiny since 1966, still remembers a childhood spent in a country stripped of everything before oil, a time when the Bedouins sucked date pits to fool their hunger. It is said that, to dispel the memories of that nightmare, he had date palms, irrigated by desalinated seawater, planted in the capital, the cities and along the main roads. Every year, at harvest time, the emirate's citizens may pick the dates for free and take as many as necessary to feed their families. At any rate, one forgets the surrounding desert, unlike Qatar and Dubai, where the sand is always present, and one has the very agreeable impression of living in the shade of an immense oasis – even if it does not stretch beyond a thin strip along the roads.

Sheikh Zayed, like his colleague Sheikh Hamed, the emir of Qatar, enjoys true popularity. The petrol boom has been placed in the service of development projects that have changed the two countries. Qatar has sacrificed the immediate enjoyment of its prosperity to some extent so that it could invest in costly gas infrastructure, which should soon allow it to play one of the very top roles worldwide in this field. Ambitious educational projects, under the aegis of Sheikha Mouza, the emir's wife and the mother of his favourite son, are growing. Private universities following American or European models, as well as cultural institutes, target first and foremost young people, who are the object of concern in all the oil states of the Arabian Peninsula.

Unlike the generation in power, which lived through the pre- and post-petrol transition, young people here have known only opulence and ease. The Emirates' Annual Review reports that 'Sheikh Zayed has long been worried about the negative effects an easy life may have on the young generation that benefits from it.' He declared: 'It is my duty, as the leader of this country's young people, to encourage them to work and make efforts to improve themselves and serve the country. Whoever is sound in mind and body yet does not work commits a crime against himself and against society.' A book in Arabic that I received in Qatar, written by two professors at the university, discusses 'deviant youth' and sums up the work of the institutions responsible for managing this problem, which seems to preoccupy the authorities greatly. In a society where sexual segregation must be observed strictly before marriage, where public higher education is not co-ed, it is difficult to reconcile this heavy tradition with the tidal wave of modernity that floods these wealthy countries with all the gadgets technology produces, and which break down all boundaries of intimacy and modesty. Young girls are dressed in black; most wear a headscarf, and often the *niqab* – a face veil that leaves only a slit open for the eyes. But that does not prevent them from gluing to their ears, even through the veil's fabric, the latest model of cell phone, its ringer's jingle tuned to techno, jazz or an Oriental riff that hardly suggests chaste conversations with a chaperone or spiritual advisor.

Boys and girls meet in the city centres, in immense air-conditioned American-style malls, giant pagan temples erected in homage to the idols of consumerism. Luxury boutiques, jewellers, shoe shops, but also, everywhere in the Gulf, Carrefour superstores with the same gondolas, trolleys and products as in the outskirts of Orléans or Marseilles. In the one in Qatar, a man in a white *dishdash* flanked by two women, their faces masked by black *niqab*s, is pushing a trolley; the group marks a long pause in front of the display of Michael Jackson's latest CD, *Invincible*, on sale at the special price of 54 Qatari riyals. Suddenly, I hear two salespeople speaking French backslang: apparently, they are young Maghrebis from France. One is at home everywhere in the global village – but the rules of the game differ from one civilization to the next. In Orléans, after meeting at Carrefour, couples gaze at each other under the romantic spotlights at McDonald's. That is impossible here: the mall's cafés each have one area for single men, and another for 'families'. There is nowhere to get to know each other and coo like pigeons. Apparently, everything happens in music stores. Groups of boys and girls seem very busy rooting about among the CDs. In fact, they are watching each other: if a promising look is exchanged, the girl will be able to find the boy's cell phone number, slipped between two albums. At the Qatar mall's skating rink, leaning on the guardrail, a little man in typical Muslim Brother garb – calf-length white *djellaba*, heavy beard, prayer callus in the middle of the forehead, white skullcap – can't take his eyes off a young Asian skater in a tight black catsuit; to the audible music on her headphones, she is mapping out graceful dance steps on the ice that highlight her body's curves.

Some of these rich, pious young people of the peninsula must have grown bored of the futile games at shopping malls and the tedium of the vast compounds, all the electronics, the automobiles and household appliances, the air-conditioning and the swimming pools, the hi-fis and the *dolce vita*. When the opportunity of *jihad* in Afghanistan against the Red Army arose in the 1980s, several hundred left on a quest for a heroism they would invent, that would reconcile defense of religion and bustard hunting, theology and falconry. All the peninsula's regimes financed this sacred combat generously. For some young people, this was just a sort of summer camp – with photos (square Afghan hat on head, combat trousers, Kalashnikov on hip) destined for pride of place in the *diwan*, the compound's reception room. Others took matters more to heart. These idle children, raised in the lap of luxury, mingled with gallows birds from Egypt or Algeria: radical partisans of the Gama'a Islamiya or Jihad, who had been involved in Sadat's assassination, then moved out in 1984 and went off to Peshawar, Islamist guerrilleros from Bouyali's gang, arrested in the maquis of the Blida Atlas and filtered out to the Pashtun mountains.

How fascinated these bumbling rich kids must have been by such seasoned militants, glorified by their time in the jails of 'apostate' leaders in Cairo or Algiers! I found some of their pictures on the Azzam Brigades' website – named after Abdallah Azzam, a Palestinian herald of the Afghan *jihad*, killed in November 1989 in an attack in Peshawar. They, too, were dead in battle, in Bosnia or Chechnya, years after the Afghan *jihad* had ended, while attempting to propagate the holy war elsewhere; and, beneath the digitized images of corpses, it was possible to read the martyr's hagiography of every *shahid*, with his *nom de guerre* followed by his regional origin.

Before they signed up to fight alongside Abdallah Azzam or Osama Bin Laden, what sort of well-brought-up children were Abu Khalid al-Qatari or Abu Hamam al-Najdi? Did they go to the shopping mall in Saudi Arabia or Qatar, and slip their telephone numbers between two CD covers, troubled by a pair of shining eyes behind the slit of a black *niqab*? Like Bin Laden himself, did they carry out the pilgrimage to liberated pre-AIDS Scandinavia to pose, like him, for a different photo next to a blonde Swede not a bit shy in her thigh-high boots and minidress? Or, like the little *djellaba*-clad man in the Qatar mall, had they simply ogled an Asian skater before going off to hunt infidels and apostates from Kashmir to Bosnia?

The Emirates Strategic Studies Centre in Abu Dhabi is an institution devoted to reflection and futurology. The furniture, like the bylaws, recalls the Council on Foreign Relations in New York, where this centre may have found its inspiration. Around the table are a few foreigners in suit and tie, and a majority of Emirates citizens in *dishdash*. The uniformity of dress is such that I have a very hard time identifying individuals as such, fixing their faces in my memory. Most wear a delicate beard, as local fashion dictates, which increases the impression of similarity. Only the cufflinks and pricey watches might allow differentiation – if one knows the brands, which is not my case. It is equally impossible, given their identical appearance, to guess the professions of those present.

The debate revolves around the eternal question: clash of civilizations or dialogue of cultures. Apparently Samuel Huntington, the author of the famous book on the 'clash', is holding a conference in Dubai, one emirate over, at this very moment. His book is a bestseller, no doubt one of the most widely available of the Western works translated into Arabic, along with the anti-Israel lampoons of Roger/Rajaa Garaudy, even in the popular libraries and on news-stands from Morocco to the Middle East. The Islamists adore him, for he brings grist to their mill: the two civilizations are incompatible; therefore the Muslim world is justified in locking itself in a radical otherness vis-à-vis the West, and the radical Islamists, who advocate the hermetic sealing of identity, in championing it ardently – *ergo* Bin Laden. I attempt to bring nuance to this brash rhetoric: in our globalized universe, the West exists in Muslim lands, and Muslims live on Western soil. This is not a war of civilizations, but a complex conflict within intertwined civilizations, which are condemned to engage in a permanent cultural dialogue, whatever the Islamists on one hand and the far right on the other might say. The Islamists are neither the end of History for Muslim societies, nor their final aim.

In the afternoon, on television, after the fall of Mazar-i Sharif and as the Northern Alliance continues to make progress, there is suddenly news of a plane crashing during take-off from New York. An attack is suspected. Accusing fingers point at Bin Laden and his group, and everyone thinks that this is revenge for the offensive that is beginning to gnaw away at Taliban lines in Afghanistan. On satellite TV, I find a French 24-hour news channel. There are blurred images of Queens, where the catastrophe took place, and stock market indices tumbling by the minute. One of the self-declared experts on terrorism, fundamentalism or Binladenism has thrown himself on a telephone to make his hot sales pitch, live. I don't know which one it is, because his face is not shown: is it the fat one, the little skinny one or the tall emaciated one, who tells everyone he was my student although I have never seen him in my life, and who exudes an extreme right-wing ideology by satellite under cover of his secondhand knowledge? Is it the 'president of the International Terrorism Observatory', the 'global consultant on fundamentalism' or another product of the same mould, with straw titles that impress gullible journalists? This one really has nothing to say. He is filling time by talking about the weather in New York. I surf towards al-Jazeera and Abu Dhabi TV.

Cheb Mami in Dubai. The idol of the French outer suburbs and the Maghreb, whose voice with its almost feminine tone causes hearts to capsize, is appearing at the airport stadium. For nothing in the world would I miss this impending clash of civilizations between North Africa and the East, *rai* and the dirges of the Orient. It takes over an hour by car along the highway, brightly lit all the way from Abu Dhabi. We go with cool friends: Beurs, Frenchies, Orientalists, Occidentalists, Franco-Lebanese ... The Cheb is coming on, but very late. It seems that this son of Oran is running errands in Dubai. We have time for dinner, while young, peroxide blonde Lebanese singers sway their hips onstage during the first act, to cries of '*ana bahibbak*!' – I love you! – like Phoenician divinities, offering up small, round, naked bellies for the faithful to adore, navels stamped with precious stones that glitter in the spotlights.

In a patio invaded by a young, joyful, cosmopolitan crowd, open-air restaurants offer an infinity of ethnic food choices. We opt for Italian-Balinese fusion, which promises to be very seductive. Prawns impaled on vertical stakes take me straight to Kuta Beach, while a heady *vino nobile* from Montepulciano brings me back to the little city perched over Tuscany, where I like to slip into the old theatre during rehearsals – in an intoxicating to-and-fro as sweeping as the great planetary traffic Dubai has set in motion. At a nearby table, a family from the Emirates is seated; the women, heads covered by fairly loose scarves, smoke a *narghileh*, releasing a scent of apples. One of them glances over a few times. Some young girls are real teases, my neighbour whispers; he knows the country well, and remarks that these affairs can end very badly. The Cheb has not filled the small stadium to capacity. Maybe the circumstances are to blame, although a feeling of complete insouciance emanates from this throng of young spectators.

Torrential rains have ravaged the popular Algiers neighbourhood of Bab al-Oued, in Cheb's country. There are many dead, carried off by the mudslides: the images of devastation are terrifying. A British newspaper has made much of Bin Laden's recent visit to a luxurious Dubai clinic – where he is said to have met a CIA agent. The authorities have denied it.

Tuesday 13 November
Last night, while we were applauding Cheb Mami, Jacques

Chirac arrived from Egypt, where he met Hosni Mubarak. This morning at around eleven, he is seeing Sheikh Zayed. The sheikh is an octogenarian, and has undergone serious kidney surgery. He receives very few visitors, and must husband his strength. But he is still the state's supreme leader. The French president wants to explain his country's position in the extreme crisis that the world and the region have been undergoing since 11 September. Of course, everyone here knows that he will be a candidate for his own replacement during the presidential elections of Spring 2002. On the occasion of the presidential visit the 'Zayed Centre for Coordination and Follow-up', a research body affiliated with the League of Arab States, is publishing a small volume of 72 pages, in Arabic. Adorned with the French president's portrait, it is titled *Jacques Chirac: Man of State and of Principles* and eulogizes his personal and political life; extols the excellence of his relations with the Arabs in general and the Emirates in particular; and predicts, given his 'great popularity' and 'all that has been achieved in France under his presidency', that his re-election is guaranteed.

In the afternoon, the French president flies off towards Saudi Arabia, where he will see King Fahd at eight. The Saudi sovereign has been laid low by an attack: he has lost the power of speech and mobility. His half-brother Prince Abdallah, the heir to the throne, is exercising kingly powers. After Abdallah, another brother, Sultan, is next in line for the crown. All are over seventy, at least – precise birth dates are not always known.

In the Peninsula's monarchies, power does not necessarily pass from father to son, but takes polygamy, and the tribal alliances that form around it, into account. This type of 'lateral' succession makes it possible to enlarge the base of supporters: each 'royal' tribe, each lineage descended from a strong mother, reckons that its turn will come, and while it waits, stands by those who hold power over the rest of the population. My brother and I against my cousin, my cousin and I against the rest of the world. But increased life expectancy and the demographic explosion have subjected this ancestral system to a difficult test. Today, it has produced a gerontocracy, and it is difficult for the generations within the governing elite to renew themselves naturally. Sometimes, as in Qatar or Oman, a son seizes the throne from his father in a palace coup, thus guarding against state sclerosis in a region where political risk is infinitely volatile and explosive, like the petrol that gushes forth here every day to supply the planet under the scrupulous surveillance of the US Army's bases and aircraft carriers.

In these rentier societies, people have procreated abundantly – like Muhammad Bin Laden, father to 53 children besides the famous Osama. Saudi Arabia today is said to house twenty million inhabitants, according to the figures in an advertorial published in the world's main newspapers this November to celebrate, with a budget of several million dollars, the twenty-year rule of a King Fahd who reigns on glossy paper, eternally young and smiling in his pictures. The manna that springs unbidden from the earth has done little to encourage devotion to labour, and the petroleum pie is now growing more slowly than the population. The royal family, with its thousands of princes big and small, helps itself first. In the traditional economy, a lord who has *nif* – honour – slaughters more sheep than necessary to feed the guests at the *meshwi*: he will win over the village by feeding it the abundant remains. The same went for oil wealth: its inexhaustible surplus stretched to the humblest Bedouins. But the demographic explosion has multiplied mouths and stomachs, and each sees his share of the banquet diminishing, until only the crumbs are left – unless one eats part of the lord's share, sits down at his table or takes his place.

In the *Declaration of Jihad Against the Americans Occupying the Land of the Two Holy Sites*, Bin Laden, who had just arrived in the Afghan mountains from Sudan in the summer of 1996, wrote a sentence few have noticed, extolling the 'great merchants of the Peninsula', commoners all, and deriding the Saudi royal family. Two years later, in a European city, a young Saudi from Jedda – the Red Sea port with a more cosmopolitan urban tradition than Riyadh, the capital – was telling me a story. His father, a liberal, and an amateur of scotch and European travel, had never shown sympathy for religious people. When he felt that he had grown old, he gathered his children around him to inform them of his will – and announced that he wished to bequeath part of his fortune to Bin Laden. His offspring were stupefied; he retorted that only he was defending the honour of their country, demeaned in his eyes to the status of mere American protectorate.

On television, one can watch the first images of Kabul's fall. The market indicator is taking off in a corner of the screen, erasing yesterday's losses. The crash in New York was an accident, apparently caused by birds sucked into the jet engine. The market has already forgotten the victims – most of them citizens of a poor Caribbean island: compensation will be much lower than if they had been Americans. The insurance companies' stocks are on the rise again. Scenes of jubilation in Kabul. Close-ups of the Afghan capital's inhabitants shaving off their beards, grinning ear-to-ear, cheeks smothered in shaving foam; others throw themselves on old second-hand television sets brought out of back shops. Kabul TV will broadcast again after five years of blackout, five years during which the only forms of public entertainment on offer were the executions of thieves and adulterers in the stadium, sinister circus games Islamist style. Once again I see the images of streets where *chadri*-clad women begged, war widows surrounded by clouds of children, forbidden from working by the zealous defenders of the *Shari'a*; I recognize the building of the Ministry of Foreign Affairs, a Soviet-style concrete parallelepiped.

Visiting Kabul under the Taliban's iron rule in the spring of 1998, I tried in vain one day to obtain an exit visa from this ministry so I could take a plane to Peshawar, Pakistan. The unkempt lawn had reverted to a primitive, verdant steppe; cannabis plants even grew there among the weeds. Perhaps it was the mythical Afghan Red the hash hippies sought most when they stopped here in the 1970s, wearing embroidered sheepskin vests, on their way to Kathmandu. Two or three Taliban, machine guns next to them, were standing guard in a debonair manner, napping by the swinging doors of this ghost ministry with empty offices, this castle where a veiled beauty slept. Some diplomats managed to flee; others, I was told, were sent to an Islamic re-education camp like the inhabitants of Phnom Penh, forced to undergo Communist re-education in the countryside after the Khmer Rouge took the city; the fruit, then, of an unlikely cousinhood between Pol Pot and Mullah Omar, two peasants' sons gripped by ideology. Only the minister was empowered to deliver an exit visa; but he rarely came to the office, no doubt preferring the intoxication of war against Commander Massoud, and did not seem to have heard of delegating signatures, an elementary administrative practice. The art of administration, however, was not taught in the *madrasa*s where the Taliban went to school. It was impossible to leave the country by airplane; on the other hand, no visa was required to cross the overland border – another mystery of the regime's administrative coherence – by taking the broken road that joins the legendary Khyber Pass via Jalalabad. That is what I did.

At every roadblock the rural Taliban, who spoke Pashtun,

mistreated the driver, a very civilized inhabitant of Kabul who spoke Dari, the form of Farsi traditional to the urban world of the capital. We had to get out of the car, wait on the shoulder and undergo unpleasant searches inflicted by sinister, brutal youngsters who smelled foul – a little like the searches to which one is subjected at Tehran Airport at the hands of the Revolutionary Guard, who hate impious foreigners. Speaking of Tehran, it took me a while to realize that the insistent suspicion I faced on this road from the intransigent defenders of Sunni Islam, despite my beard, arose from an unfortunate misunderstanding. Tanned, brown-haired, wearing dark trousers and jacket, I was taken for an Iranian – and the terrible hatred they harboured for the Shi'ite they suspected me of being triumphed over their banal detestation of an infidel. The driver was terrified; the bumpkins with Kalashnikovs made the Kabuli pay for his urbanity and polite manners. We had five flat tires before Jalalabad, and fixed the shreds of rubber torn by the road's sharp stones in shops with no electricity, amidst a grandiose landscape of vertiginous mountains, then in a valley planted as far as the eye could see with poppies, their delicate flowers red and white, cultivated for the opium that enriched the Islamist regime while rotting the fibre of the West's youth.

In Jalalabad, we had to change cars, as one changed horses at a coaching inn in the olden days. The new driver was a true-blue Pashtun, very comfortable with the Taliban who controlled the checkpoints – maybe members of his tribe, or another one

Middle Ages and lolloped, eyes bulging, before the television cameras; no more images of Bin Laden on a white horse, no more on-the-spot recordings of his declarations! Welcome back Christiane Amanpour, her jet-black helmet of hair, CNN's Atlanta studio, the familiar male and female busts, the ads for major hotel chains, Business News, Money Line, Q & A!

This substitution seems to me to be more important than the Afghan capital's surrender properly speaking. Once again, America's voice will be able to tell History, produce it, give events the meaning it wishes and transmit that to the world as a whole. For the first time in the contemporary period, the major account of History-in-the-making was narrated by a voice and in a language that did not belong to the West. This was done in Arabic, and by news professionals like the others. CNN was reduced to buying al-Jazeera's images. Many condemned this channel, which gave Bin Laden a chance to speak, and diffused his message. But in an open society, it is necessary to know how to hear a plurality of discourses, to vanquish others through the force of one's arguments, not through censorship. This voice from the East will be silent no longer, and it will enrich our perception of the world. I switch to al-Jazeera to see what is on the screen. A report from Tehran, a sidewalk poll of passersby and their satisfaction at the fall of Kabul, and another in Islamabad, where sentiments are divided. Images of Algiers, devastated by torrential rains, the inhabitants' anger with their leaders. Apparently the floods have caused such extensive

Pakistanis from England who are going to Saudi Arabia – they must have caught a connection in Paris, on their way from Manchester or Birmingham. They are wearing traditional outfits, which the young ones have donned over jeans and Fila trainers. They seem to come from a modest background, and even those who are in their twenties speak English very poorly. Perhaps this is a consequence of the discrepant development today's British education system has bred, with its exaltation of community differences. One of them is wearing the same small square bonnet, cut high on the forehead, as the Taliban in the middle of the big photo illustrating an article in today's *Libé*, about the Northern Alliance troops' siege of Kunduz. The group moves around quite a bit, and has been seated on a row near an exit, facing the flight attendant's jump seat, where the burliest of the crew members – perhaps a mere coincidence – is sitting and conversing with them. They speak about football, the French players in England, the latest matches, sports in general, hobbies. One of the youths smiles, showing a gold incisor: 'Me, I like drive planes, I train!' The flight attendant replies: 'Small planes?' 'No, big planes, Boeing, Airbus!' The others burst out laughing before the flight attendant, having grasped the allusion, retorts that it is not funny, and resumes control of the conversation.

The Muslim passengers coming from England have all requested special *halal* meals, with meat from cattle ritually slaughtered under the control of a butcher accredited by a mosque. But they send them back and request that they be kept warm, because it is still daylight, and the *muezzin* has not announced the end of the Ramadan fast. In principle, however, the dispositions of fasting do not apply to travellers – behind me two women, middle-aged Maghrebis on their way to Jedda, heads covered, are eating an ordinary meal and chatting away in *Franco-Arabe*. Instead of a *muezzin*, it is the cabin chief who will make an announcement to the 'Muslim passengers' that it is time for *iftar*: Air France has become an authority in religious matters, an aspect of the national company's privatization that had heretofore escaped me. I do not know whose time it is following: the Mosquée de Paris, al-Azhar, Mecca? After all, we are in the sky and I can still see the sun on the horizon through the porthole. Or perhaps an in-house imam sends airborne planes the signal from the control tower?

But all this is unimportant, because we have begun our descent towards Cairo, seatbelts are fastened and the meals can no longer be served. Leaving the airport, dusk has finally fallen. Over the city, deserted because people are breaking their fast, wafts a very discreet perfume of ripe guavas. I know where I am once more. Almost thirty years ago, at night, I rode in an unlit third-class train between Aswan and Luxor which ran so slowly that people travelled on the roof to taste the evening coolness, and peasants with crates of fruit to sell the passengers could board while the train was in motion. The darkness perfumed itself with heavy gusts from very ripe guavas, whispers were heard along with the chanting of an Oriental singer from a transistor radio in a far-off carriage; from that moment on, I understood that I would love Egypt in a way that, despite the vicissitudes, has never failed. I will return to the upper Nile Valley for Christmas this year.

Saturday 24 November

The newspaper stand on Soliman Pasha Street, in front of the Groppi coffee shop – a mere shadow of its former splendour – sells all sorts of 'instant books' about Bin Laden. In Arabic, too, as in the West, these are being published: cut-and-paste jobs from the Internet, which serve as substitutes for real works and try to take advantage of readers in the heat of the moment. The proliferation of these empty promises goes hand in hand with the invasion of the small screen and column inches by counterfeiters who have signed these pseudo-books and feed their twaddle to journalists who are in a rush, and not very particular. To buttress their imposture and conquer market shares, they even inveigh against academic Orientalists, try them for witchcraft with the complicity of a few publications eager for scandals that will guarantee high circulation, and work to deliver them to popular spite. My colleagues and I went through a lot after 11 September! Without bothering to read our books, the pack howled: what, analysing the decline of Islamism? Are our dear professors just nimbus clouds at best, unless they are sold? 'Perched atop his conceptual minaret', pronounced one diagnostician of my case, an amateur novelist who imagines he has style; 'so you were wrong, right?' demanded another; 'false prophet!' shouted a third, as eager in slander as he was only yesterday in sycophancy. The clamour stopped short with the fall of Kabul, the Taliban debacle, the hunt for Bin Laden. The pack, suddenly stunned, disbanded, tails between legs. Some may be thinking that they will have to read the professors' books and try to understand them. What if they were not wrong after all? So many pages, such small print! How many headaches to look forward to ... Here, sirs, no hard feelings: here, for your penance and edification, is this brief travel account.

Sunday 25 November

At Cairo University, I meet the students with whom I had debated before the fall of Kabul. The Bin Laden side has collapsed, even among the denim-clad teenyboppers who find him adorable. Too bad for the losers.

With a former student from Paris, we visit the 'Ramadan tables'. In Arabic, they are called '*ma'idat al-Rahman*' – literally, 'the table of the Merciful' – one of the attributes of God, 'Most Gracious, Most Merciful', according to the established formula. In previous years, during which a rapidly enriched bourgeoisie proliferated in Egypt while the people – endlessly swollen by the demographic explosion – were growing poorer, these 'tables' multiplied. This was especially so in the nouveau riche neighbourhood of Mohandessin ('Engineers'), lined with graceless buildings where vast apartments are furnished in 'Louis Farouk' style – a hybrid of uncertain taste between Louis XV and Turkish delight. Set up in front of the garish plate-glass windows of big German car dealers, pricey furniture shops, Islamic banks and mosques covered in marble and larded with raw green neon lights, these free meals are for the poor, who come to break their fast at the expense of a benefactor whose name is clearly inscribed on the next shopfront. My rambling companion, who has written an article about this phenomenon and is following its evolution, remarks that they are far less numerous this year than last. Is this a sign of the recession that is hitting the entire region so hard, and will grow worse with the dwindling flow of tourists after the September attacks? Or a desire for discretion on the part of certain Islamic financial groups and other businessmen, at a time when several of them are the targets of investigations, under suspicion of having channelled funds to Bin Laden and his organization? There is a placid police presence around the locations; the *shawish*es – little policemen dressed in black – are holding flasks so that they can break their fast without leaving their positions. This year, for the first time, most of the tables are hidden from view by vast swathes of brightly patterned cloth, as if one ought not to watch the poor eating out of a sort of diffidence.

We go to *Nadi al-Sayd*, the 'Shooting Club', where on Friday the new bourgeois meet, since they have no access to the *Nadi al-Gezira*, the Gezira Sporting Club, reserved for the old families. The club features a mosque where a very trendy young preacher, Amr Khaled, has built himself such a reputation that he now poses a threat to pop stars. Held in low regard by al-Azhar's *ulema*, some of whom call him a 'sheikh-show', he advocates amassing wealth and punctuates his sermons with references to the latest cell phone or luxury automobile. He is very much in demand in the private schools where the pious middle class sends its offspring. A specialized firm, which one contacts by telephone, takes care of marketing his cassette tapes. Opposite the entrance to the 'Shooting Club', huge tables are spread to serve several hundred. The meal trays must have been borrowed from the cafeteria of a company or university. The people in charge do not want to speak to us: orders have been given. One of the waiters takes me aside. He asks me if I can get him a visa to Germany. I tell him I am French, but he replies that it does not matter, that now there are visas valid for all the Union's countries, that he is not interested in France, that he wants to go to Germany, to Hamburg, where there is work. Where has he formed such a positive image of Germany, which is hardly perceived as a European Eldorado these days? An old reputation, perhaps; unless it is the renown gained by Muhammad Atta, the Egyptian pilot of the first plane that crashed into the World Trade Center, who spent a long time as a student in Hamburg?

Two Egyptian friends have made us dinner. One is a TV journalist, the other is completing her studies. They are from a very humble background. They were veiled; one has taken it off for good, the other still puts it on to go out. They speak no foreign languages, but are curious about everything that is going on in the world. We speak a lot, for a very long time. The scene reminds me of passages from Stratis Tsirkas's beautiful novel *Drifting Cities*, which is set in Egypt and Palestine during the Second World War. In it, young Oriental women flee their suffocating condition through dialogue with Europeans. They do not really know what they want to do with their lives. Try to emigrate? Perhaps, but it is so difficult to get a visa.

On a low table, there are glossy English-language publications: *Cleo – Egypt's Modern Lifestyle Magazine*; *Enigma – Egypt's Magazine for the New Millennium*; *Egypt's Insight*. They have only been around for four or five years; I didn't know about them. On the cover are young local models, men or women, very beautiful and sexy. These magazines are published in Cyprus, where they benefit from offshore press licences. Much of the content is given over to photos of receptions in big hotels, marriages, various celebrations, a sort of hypertrophied people section where polite society laughs to see itself so beautiful in this mirror ... They also contain 'organic' or 'low-cal' recipes for breaking the fast without gaining too much weight in this month of Ramadan, when the rich take *iftar* as a pretext to gorge limitlessly and gain unsightly origin, including those who have acquired citizenship. This mentality does not seem to bode well for dialogue, in my view.

Today's press is not much more nuanced. One daily recounts, with triumphal overtones, that the Italian ambassador to Saudi Arabia has converted to Islam. I do not know if the diplomat was overcome by the superiority of the faith, or fell for a Muslim woman he wanted to marry. True, the episode is comical in light of Prime Minister Berlusconi's declarations regarding the superiority of Christian and Western civilization, but as long as each conversion is counted as another step towards Islam's planetary victory, dialogue will be difficult. The unfortunate man, we will learn later, has been recalled to Farnesina for consultations ... As for the American ambassadors, they simper away as the offensive against the Taliban and Bin Laden continues in Afghanistan. The one posted to Pakistan has let it be known that she fasts during Ramadan; the one in Paris organizes an *iftar*, carefully *halal*, for all his colleagues from Muslim countries, while George Bush, Jr, having declared a 'crusade' of good against evil, goes into a Washington mosque wearing his socks. It would be funny if it were not so sad.

While the Arab League works on, I go to visit a lawyer, Montasser al-Zayyat. A former radical Islamist, jailed for several years, he has specialized in defending incarcerated militants. In 1996–97, he played a pivotal role in convincing the

Egyptian Gama'a Islamiyya and Jihad activists to renounce violence. He is a corpulent man, his hair dyed black but his beard salt-and-pepper. He greets me very courteously. In Afghanistan, things are turning sour for the 'Arab Afghans', the *jihad* brigades who make up the bulk of Bin Laden's troops. They have tumbled out of the villas requisitioned in Afghanistan's cities, leaving behind their belongings and many documents that should dispel many mysteries regarding al-Qa'ida's terrorist saga if they are utilized.

Montasser al-Zayyat estimates around 2,000 Arabs are still in the war zone, at least a quarter of them Egyptian. Most are stuck there, since no government wants them – unlike the Algerians, who returned home massively between 1989 and 1992, took advantage of the anarchy of the FIS years, then built up the GIA and contributed efficiently to the atrocious bloodbath of the Algerian civil war according to methods taught in the anti-Soviet training camps by Pakistani special services under CIA auspices. But most of the Egyptians must have stayed put – those who came home in 1992 to wage *jihad* and massacre tourists were mowed down or, when they were arrested, condemned and executed. Today, the core Taliban, to recover their political virginity, retrieve tribal honour and smooth their transformation into honest pro-American Pashtuns, are abandoning the Arabs when they are not selling them. The hatred the Afghans felt for them, the televised images of the Northern Alliance's Arab prisoners beaten and bound, have spread shock waves among those who had swallowed the propaganda of Muslim solidarity against imperialism, and defended the besieged Taliban as brothers in religion attacked by the infidels.

In a recent article in the Beirut daily *al-Nahar*, a Lebanese intellectual, Samir Kassir, after noting that in Kabul today the term 'Arab' no longer has any positive connotations, deplores the fact that 'Arab intellectuals have ceaselessly justified the Arab street's sympathy for Bin Laden and the Taliban in the face of the American attack'. He hopes that the fall of the 'emirate of Afghanistan' holds a lesson in freedom that will allow the Arabs to find the path to rebirth. These images of a Muslim people's joy in Kabul liberated from the Taliban, the Afghans' rage against the Arab combatants, Montasser al-Zayyat explains, are terrible, and will provoke very profound uncertainty. I assume he is referring only to the *jihadi* militants, but he corrects me: the Islamist trend as a whole is involved.

Emerging from the lawyer's office, I arrive on Opera Square – named after the opera house that Empress Eugénie inaugurated, built almost at the same time as the Opéra de Paris. The building burnt down, and was replaced by a multi-storey garage. On a street not far from here, in this old colonial quarter emptied of its European population over the years, lived Muhammad Atta, the pilot of that first plane. The photo published in the newspapers during the first week of October struck me. It was taken by one of those professional photographers everyone is mad about in the Orient, where one poses against an interchangeable backdrop representing a landscape – usually a view of Europe or America, snowy mountains, verdant Swiss valleys, the skyline of a famous city. The Attas chose a birch forest, the thin trunks forming a sort of inextricable net in the background. This projection into the dream of a European forest is in sharp contrast to the fine city clothes parents and children are wearing, but also underlines the European character of their get-up. The father, tall, in three-piece suit and tie, is looking into the camera triumphantly, proud of an achievement we do not know about. By his sides are the mother and son. She is bent over her child and has taken his face in her hands, the better to cover him in kisses, perhaps, or to bring him out, make him the centre of the picture. The child is Muhammad Atta, the future pilot who will be charged after 11 September with having caused several thousand deaths. He seems indifferent to this overprotective mother. He might be twelve. Like his daddy, he is looking into the camera, but seems more intimidated. He is wearing a shirt and trousers, held up by suspenders over a fat little tummy.

A Brief Chronicle of Israel
and Palestine

Saturday 28 April 2001

Nazareth. A forest of red flags has peacefully invaded the main street of the old Arab city in Nazareth. The procession, led by the city's mayor and the Democratic Front's Knesset deputies, wends its way around the kitsch Basilica of the Annunciation and the parking lot below. The Islamist movement's militants have put up green banners there to mark the site of the mosque they want to build in front of the church, and which will hide it from view. Here, as elsewhere, every square metre of Holy Land belongs to whoever can shout the loudest to impose his eternal rights. In Nazareth's municipal elections, the Islamist list was almost even with the Front – close to the Communists – which barely kept the mayor's office, and whose troops are parading today, four days early, to celebrate 1 May. They are taking advantage of its being Saturday – the Sabbath, a holiday in Israel, unlike Labour Day – to bring together the maximum number of militants, especially employees and young students. They are only a few thousand, amidst the sarcastic remarks of the bearded shopkeepers, whose stalls are adorned with the portrait of Hasan al-Banna, founder of the Muslim Brotherhood in Egypt in the 1920s. The parade is preventing Jewish immigrants from the former USSR, momentarily frightened, from coming to buy fruits and vegetables from these stalls, which sell them cheaper than the supermarkets. I do not remember seeing so many red flags in the Arab world in decades. The young girls are pretty, wreathed in smiles, their arms bare in white cotton t-shirts printed with Che Guevara's picture, red scarves around their necks. Their long black hair floats in the wind, like a challenge to the women in synthetic veils who pass indifferently on the footpaths, surrounded by gaggles of children. Everything indicates that they belong to an Arab-Israeli middle class, where secular Christians and Muslims guard their threatened co-existence behind the incantation of the Communist movement's obsolete slogans. A float bears the cardboard ruins of a house destroyed by a missile that is stamped with a Star of David and the American flag. The children are carrying signs inscribed with the name and age of Palestinian children killed during the most recent Intifada, which began in autumn of 2000. Others are calling for a Palestinian state with holy Jerusalem (al-Quds al-sharif) as its capital. In the forest of red banners, a streamer in Hebrew, borne by sandal-wearing Ashkenazi communists in their sixties, is topped by a Palestinian and an Israeli flag. This is the first time since the al-Aqsa Intifada began – and the bullets of the

Israeli police killed thirteen Arab Israelis – that the blue and white flag of the Hebrew State has been flown in a demonstration, side by side with the Palestinian flag. That is most probably why it is necessary to dilute them in the mass of red flags.

In front of the al-Salam Mosque, controlled by the most radical branch of the Islamist movement (which refuses to participate in Knesset elections), packets of rice, flour and tomato paste are lined up, the result of donations that minivans equipped with loudspeakers solicit constantly, criss-crossing the Sabbath-empty streets crushed by the *khamasin*'s heat. Israel's Muslim believers – whose income level is far superior to that of the Palestinians – are especially ready to give to their brothers on the other side of the Green Line because none would exchange his living conditions for theirs. The young imam at the mosque with the long, thick black beard, his cell phone always within reach, drives us to his village facing Mount Thabor. To reach it, we cross the shiny Jewish city of Nazareth Illit, on the heights, whence armed civilians descended during the last Intifada. A young Arab Israeli died very near the mosque, one of the martyrs whose portrait adorns the posters on the walls. Every day the imam commutes in his air-conditioned car, driving through the olive groves seized by the Hebrew State, where the kibbutz's uniformly similar houses – solar panels on every roof – are lined up. The kibbutz has welcomed many Jews from the former Soviet Union during this past decade, during

103

which the Holy Land's Orthodox churches apparently have also experienced an influx of new parishioners. The imam, whose young children unceremoniously mingle in the conversation, avoids the term 'Arab Israeli', preferring that of '1948 Arab'. While justifying his refusal to participate in Knesset elections – as against the other, minority tendency in the Islamist movement, which has sent deputies to the Israeli parliament and succumbed to the delicious traps of co-option – he nevertheless makes it clear that, within the framework of Israeli 'pseudo-democracy' (*shibh al-dimuqratiyya*), he can say whatever he pleases in his sermon; and, if he had said a tenth of it in any Arab countries, he would have had a rough time. But Israel is still a state that treats its citizens differently according to religious identity, he notes: thus the ultra-religious Sephardic Shaas party, whose rabbis and leaders make statements no less scandalous and communitarian than our own imam's, benefits from hefty subsidies while his payment is limited to donations from the faithful.

Has the violence of the Intifada in autumn, and the Arab Israeli victims, created an internal front, as some in Tel Aviv and Arab capitals are saying, and burned bridges between the Hebrew State and its non-Jewish citizens? A little over six months after the events, it seems first that they have allowed for the political negotiations between the two parties to be pushed up a notch: the Arab side makes more demands, while the Jewish side feigns wanting to concede less. In this field as in many others, Mr Sharon's government, clinging to the discourse of security alone, has yet to make any political choices.

Sunday 29 April

After the Sabbath and the national holiday, the Haifa-Jerusalem highway via Tel Aviv is one long traffic jam full of busloads of soldiers on leave returning to their barracks, rifles slung across their shoulders. These are the same buses targeted by Palestinian kamikazes, in operations for which only the Islamists of Hamas and Jihad claim responsibility. The north of Tel Aviv, Natanya and Herzliah have experienced exceptional economic development in the past few years. This is the heart of the local Silicon Valley, which generates considerable profits, futurist buildings in glass and steel, American-style malls and trendy cafés where yuppies with or without kippas sip espresso, their cell phones at their ears. We are far from Nazareth, very far from Ramallah, light-years from Gaza, where the bombers probably come from. Still, I am told that many of these brilliant young creators, whose skills are better recompensed in America or Europe, are beginning to leave for climes where they do not run the risk of dying in a terrorist attack.

To the naked eye, Israel has become a 'multicultural' society – or a postmodern one, if you prefer. In the bus stuck in traffic next to mine, a young Falasha girl in uniform with a delicate black face and abundant hair pulled into a ponytail is carrying on an inaudible dialogue with her neighbour, whose features are Slavic and who is also in uniform, her blonde mane falling to her shoulders. The Jerusalem bus station is yet another world: the streets are crawling with religious men dressed in black, faces white and pimply; the women, in wigs and hats, are pregnant for the most part, with litanies of children clinging to their skirts. On the neighbourhood's trilingual road signs, the Arabic indications have been defaced with black paint. Is the Zionist melting pot still capable of mingling all these populations, or is each pursuing its separate development?

Monday 30 April

At the end of a symposium at the Hebrew University in Jerusalem, Avi Pazner, Ariel Sharon's spokesman and one of the most hawkish Francophone Israelis, attacks the French ambassador to Tel Aviv, takes ritual offense at De Gaulle's 1967 'betrayal' and prays for a 're-balancing' of French policy in the region. Professor Zeev Sternheel, whose French is slightly tinged with a southern accent – a souvenir from his years spent hiding from the Nazis in the Midi – mocks the cuckold's eternal lament that Israel addresses to France and invites his compatriots to look squarely at a situation where the stronger never wins universal sympathy. Beyond the hyperbole and rhetoric, beyond Israel's crushing military superiority – it is capable of leading so-called 'surgical' warfare of the Gulf War or Kosovo variety – against regional adversaries that the USSR's disappearance and their own social backwardness have deprived of comparative means of retaliation, one feels a muffled anxiety for the medium term. When the euro comes into force, Israel, like the Middle East as a whole, will shift, due to the weight of commercial exchanges, into a monetary zone requiring that it establish political relations with the EU. These have been neglected so far, in favour of a single Israeli-American axis. The Hebrew State is late, and is having difficulty putting its point across convincingly. The Sharon-Peres government has not presented any political projects, or even a perspective around which to recommence peace talks; it has defined no stakes beyond security. It is playing for time, faced with a Palestinian Authority enfeebled by sanctions, which it hopes to bring to heel. But this is only a tactic, and the Israeli academic-political establishment is wondering anxiously whether Sharon really does have a strategy. If the Bush administration, whose secretary of state has announced his readiness to 'assist' without 'insisting', seems happy to accommodate this tactic, for now at least, and concentrate on the American common market, the same cannot be said of the European states bordering the Mediterranean: for them, peace in the region is a crucial stake. And in Europe, whose role must necessarily grow, France is the Mediterranean chief; hence the Hebrew State's interest in making up for lost time, by re-establishing links with access, networks and support it has never cultivated, heaping sarcasm, reproaches and curses upon them until very recently.

Tuesday 1 May

In his Ramallah office, Yasser Arafat, relaxed and smiling, jokes in Egyptian dialect. There is no longer any trace of the tremors that affected his lip and hindered his movements. Only his white, almost diaphanous skin betrays age and the attrition of power, behind the thick glasses he puts on to sign the documents an aide-de-camp brings in throughout the interview. The ink flowing from the presidential pen is the main line linking the Palestinian Authority to the society living in the autonomous territories, the West Bank and Gaza. This is one of the main points of criticism one hears in Palestine: the institutions the Authority has set up – ministries, parliament, etc – have little weight when compared to access to the president and the ink flowing from his pen, the decisive criterion in an individual's political influence. Arafat incarnates Palestine; he is its symbol (*ramz*) according to the slogans on walls in the occupied territories wishing him a long life. The absence of an institutionalized, pluralist political life is the Achilles' heel of the system of Palestinian autonomy, one of the reasons that led it into the dead end of the al-Aqsa Intifada.

To our question on his vision for the near future, the Authority's chairman responds that a more active role for Europe and the US is urgently needed, and that he is willing to recommence peace talks, which depend only on the Israeli prime minister's determination. To hear him develop this argument and insist on the hassles, frustrations and obstacles

Israel puts up to make daily life unbearable for the Palestinians, one feels that the autumn uprising has not accomplished much – apart from bringing Ariel Sharon to power. Many of those who deplore the death of the Oslo process refuse to see that it only fulfilled the function its signatories gave it at the time, and that it is now – to use a term popular in the region – 'bankrupt'. Israel wanted one main advantage from Oslo: to pull its young conscripts out of the Gaza soup, where they were mired in policing operations whose political, social and human cost had become too high. Arafat, confronted with Hamas's spectacular increase in popularity – its leaders, deported to Lebanon, were monopolizing the international media – needed an ace to regain the upper hand. The autonomy of the fragmented territories of Gaza and the West Bank, moth-eaten by Israeli colonies, snipped to shreds by throughways, with Tsahal in control of the lookout points, was his last card. His Arab and Palestinian adversaries condemned them as Bantustans. On the ground, the image is not off the mark; but it overlooks the Palestinians' irrepressible aspiration to return to their land, the power of the symbolic satisfaction there was in that hope and the undeniable political dividends Arafat reaped. He regained hegemony over his Islamist adversaries, later duly called to heel by the Palestinian security services armed to that end by the international community. In 2000 the terms of the process were in place: the Palestinian Authority was policing Gaza, and Hamas's dynamism was crushed. But in the longer term, the

for the Israeli army. With eight months of hindsight, the uprising's principal effect was to precipitate the fall of Ehud Barak, a victim of his own false calculations, against an adversary brought to power by a large majority of Israelis convinced that dialogue was no longer possible as long as the Palestinians were demanding the right of return for the refugees who fled in 1948 – a demand these voters perceive as the pure and simple negation of Israel's existence as a Zionist state with secure, recognized borders.

With a few nuances, the young generation of Palestinian politicians privately accepts this way of thinking. The Intifada could not be an end in itself – rather, it is a means of emerging from the political impasse created by the Oslo process's bankruptcy. On the Palestinian side, it seems clear enough that dismantling the colonies is at stake in the coming negotiations, one of the keys to minimal viability for the territory the Authority controls. But it is very difficult to make out over just what the Sharon government is willing to negotiate. Nevertheless, it will be necessary to find a common object for negotiations, for the current situation cannot last forever. It is weakening all the potential peace partners, and in the long term will strengthen peace's enemies in each camp.

After the interview with Arafat, we go to see the site of the attack that destroyed a house the previous night, a few hundred metres away from his office, killing a Fatah cadre and two children from another family. The building has collapsed inward, without damaging the surrounding structures: a 'surgical' operation. The previous day, in the Arab city of Umm al-Fahm, in Israel, two people speaking Arabic opened fire on a young Jew, killing him instantly.

Wednesday 2 May

To reach Ramallah from Birzeit University, it is necessary to cross a Tsahal checkpoint. This morning, the traffic is endless, and many of the cars are turning back. The West Bank middle class, which rather believed in the peace process, is the special target of Israeli acts of revenge. In Ramallah, one can only live freely in a few square kilometres. A permit is necessary to go to Jerusalem; lengthy and difficult to obtain, such permits are given out meanly, even for 'VIPs'. Towards Birzeit and Nablus, they depend on the whim of the soldiers who control the checkpoints located in the 'B' zone, where Israel exercises its military authority.

'Would you prefer us to throw stones, sand or flowers?' At Birzeit University, cordial irony greets the first French national to hold a conference – on Islamist movements, yet – since one of his illustrious compatriots, Lionel Jospin, had stones thrown at him after a few words on Lebanese Hizbullah that did not go down too well. The auditorium is astonishingly receptive to an analysis based on political sociology, not at all militant and eager for information and debate, far from the conspiracy theories that are the norm on many campuses in the Arab world today. The premises are very well kept: there are no grafitti or posters apart from the regulation signboards. We could almost be at Sciences Po. 'Birzeit is no longer what it used to be,' says a young colleague sadly. 'When we were students, everyone was militant. Now they don't care. They want to learn, and find jobs. Politics is out. Students don't believe in it anymore.' There is only a minority of bearded men and veiled women on campus – some of the women heavily made up, one wearing quite suggestive sand-coloured overalls with a matching scarf.

Back to Jerusalem. In the madly retro lobby of the King David Hotel, a few American Jews in shorts and kippas are moping about wearily. Tourism has come to a virtual halt since the beginning of the Intifada, and suites with a view on the old city walls can be had for next to nothing.

Thursday 3 May

The grafitti hits you first in Gaza. It exists in the West Bank too (except at Birzeit), but in Gaza it covers every available surface with scrupulous calligraphy, no matter what the political tendency, as if on this strip of earth, sunk in massive unemployment since the Intifada began, there was all the time in the world to write on walls. In terms of numbers, Hamas's slogans win hands down. Besides the usual Islamist slogans – all directed against Israel, they avoid mentioning Arafat and the PA – there are many murals. So much political iconography is unusual in a Sunni land, and is rather reminiscent of Tehran or the southern suburbs of Beirut. Big portraits of Sheikh Yassin – Hamas's spiritual guide – of 'Engineer' Yehia Ayyash, the activist killed by his booby-trapped cell phone and of Che Guevara, acclimatized in this landscape by his beard (and Lebanese family origins?), border on more explicit representations of the Islamist movement's understanding of the Intifada. Buses stamped with the Star of David explode in pools of blood. A giant brandishing a dagger with a Palestine-shaped blade prepares to kill a half-suffocated Israeli soldier, tongue hanging out, above a slogan glorifying the Ezzedin Qassam Brigades, the armed branch of the Islamist movement named after an activist sheikh.

The other striking thing, in Gaza, is the presence of animals. Horse-drawn carts and harnessed donkeys weighed down with goods are common. They point to the general poverty of the territory, encircled by sea and barbed wire; its small size; and the capacity, unique to animals, to slip with their burdens through the narrow streets of the refugee camps where the modern constraints of a typical slum have met the medina's traditional urbanist gesture – its dead-end streets, tortuous alleys and the social organization of promiscuity. Z. is around thirty – even if he looks twenty years older. A construction worker, he has not worked in Israel since the events began, and is unemployed. Two years ago, he had four children. Now he has six, and his young wife, a white scarf on her head, is pregnant with the seventh. The UN Refugee Works Agency gives them 120 shekels per child every three months, as well as rations – sugar, rice, etc – on which the family subsists. The children eat off a metal tray placed on the dirt floor, under the tin roof. They are sunk in contemplation of al-Jazeera on the satellite television. The eldest is playing with the options on his father's latest-model cell phone. The conversation touches on politics, the situation, disillusionment with all those who only shout slogans so they can appear on television but do not change anything at all. Gaza has one of the highest birth rates in the world, and children represent a way of insuring the future, a sort of equilibrium in poverty. In the immediate term, they bring in food; later, they will give their father a little money from their menial jobs; and finally, they will take charge of their ageing parents in the absence of any health insurance or pension fund. This galloping demography haunts Israel, which has no rejoinder to the cradle *jihad*. Z.'s wife confides that she would have liked to stop having children. Uneducated, unemployed, she has no say in the matter.

Mohamed Dahlan, the head of Palestinian security in Gaza, along with his counterpart Jibril Rajoub on the West Bank, is one of the key answers to the question of Arafat's eventual successor. For the time being, he holds Gaza. In fact, no tension can be felt in this city, and no animosity towards the (very infrequent) foreigners. He offers a nuanced reply to those who warned us that the Islamist movement would rise irrepressibly and the PA weakened if Europe and the US did not pressure

Israel to negotiate. Hamas, in its Gaza bastion, has the right to exist as long as it obeys the rules of the political game. The movement belonged to the Intifada Coordination Committee but did not play a decisive role, and everyone knows it. Its capacities are limited. On the other hand, he cannot comprehend the Israeli attitude. He, who guarantees security in the Strip, was shot at after his most recent meeting with Israeli officers, at the Erez checkpoint. Yet it is very clear that he plays no part in operations inside Israeli territory. The home-made explosives and bus kamikazes are not the weapons his forces use; if they decided to act, they would resort to far more elaborate methods.

Ismail Abu Shanab, an engineer, wears the Islamist trend's regulation full beard (despite his name, which in Arabic means 'the one with the mustache'), and welcomes us into his home dressed in the white *djellaba* customary in this milieu. He is one of Hamas's political leaders, trained in the US, with a very clear mind that expresses itself in elegant, persuasive Arabic. Like his colleague, the Nazareth imam, he is past master in oratory rhetoric. Similarly, too, he is interrupted during the discussion by his young children's embraces. What about operations inside Israeli territory, the suicide bombings that kill civilians? The movement recognizes them and accepts responsibility. The rule of an eye for an eye holds against the Israeli army, which does not hesitate to kill Palestinian civilians, including children; and this is the only way of pressuring the Hebrew State to stop its exactions. If Israel is an enemy, Arafat and the PA, for their part, are political adversaries; the combat is of a different nature. By not participating in the elections to the Palestinian parliament, Hamas marked its refusal to back the political system that emerged from peace accords it does not recognize any more than it does the Israeli state's existence. Palestine stretches 'from the sea to the [Jordan] river', and the struggle aims to recover it in its entirety. The Jews who choose to live there will be able to do so according to the rules Islamic law prescribes. As for the PA, it has taken stock of the dead end into which peace negotiations led it. That is why it triggered the al-Aqsa Intifada. Even if Hamas did not play the primary role, the uprising adjusted itself to Hamas's policies, and today the movement is the most deeply rooted in society, thanks to its mutual assistance networks. As is the case for all the groups descended from the Muslim Brotherhood, winning over society is the necessary preliminary to taking political power.

Social networking and control of charity associations are crucial political stakes in Gaza, where a large part of the population lives off assistance and subsidies. The UN's specialized agency, UNRWA, only distributes aid within the refugee camps. The PA, through its Ministry of Social Affairs, explains the minister, Mrs Intisar al-Wazir – the widow of Abu Jihad, the PLO's 'number two' killed in Tunis by the Mossad shortly after the first Intifada began – distributes assistance chiefly to the 'martyrs' families', who receive a sort of military or civil pension according to rank, the family's situation, etc. Thus, a civilian victim's family immediately receives 2,000 dollars, plus 600 shekels (around 170 euros) every month. All this is duly centralized by a computerized accounting system. Controlling the funds provided by the various charity associations, in this context, is the key to constituting clienteles for the different movements squabbling over the population's allegiance. The PA's budget has declined dramatically since the second Intifada began. European aid helped make ends meet, while Arab aid, for the time being, is restricted to extravagant promises.

With regard to the Islamists' charitable activities, it is impossible to lay hold of a budget or even an estimate. Dr Mahmoud Zahhar, Hamas's figurehead and a physician to the poor who receives us in his clinic after hours, maintains that the assistance his movement distributes is provided exclusively by donations from the faithful – in contrast to those who believe that a large part of the funding comes from the Arabian Peninsula and humanitarian Islamist NGOs. Everything is decided at the mosque: that is where people come to make their needs known; then those in charge send out 'inspectors', who evaluate the degree of need and classify the petitioner in one of three categories: those who deserve regular subsidies, those who receive irregular assistance according to circumstance and finally those who can participate in an investment chosen as socially productive. Each mosque has a list of its faithful, their contact information and their needs, according to a system of community policing that guarantees the movement's rootedness.

Day is drawing to a close over Gaza. Past the Erez checkpoint, amid the Jewish colonies, as the sun disappears behind the dunes, two shells explode, followed by a storm of machine-gun fire – the evening routine in this low-intensity Intifada. From Ashkelon, in Israeli territory, a taxi driver from Djerba takes me towards Tel Aviv. In Ashkelon, there is not much for young people to do. A few weeks ago, in the shopping centre from which the taxi departed, on the eve of the Sabbath, there was apparently a violent fight between two gangs, one Ethiopian, the other Russian. Something about a girl. The driver speaks of Sarcelles, where part of his family lives.

Friday 4 May

Tel Aviv. Brunch in a trendy café where no one has ever seen an Arab or a religious Jew, or perhaps even a Falasha. This could be San Francisco, or the Bastille. It is difficult, in one week and so few kilometres, to cross so many interlocked, dissimilar and antagonistic universes. What are these half-naked young people thinking as they sip their mimosas? Are they worried that their government will have to negotiate sooner or later? Are they thinking that a Hamas kamikaze could suddenly arrive in their midst, as the authorities never tire of repeating?

A ritual search and an interminable interrogation await at Lod Airport – always complicated for someone with Arab visas on his passport: 'Why did you go to Sudan? Why did you go to Gaza? Did you meet any local people there?'

The 80 shekels still in my pocket at the airport's bookstore will serve to purchase a thriller titled *Saturday Morning Crime*. The plot is set in Jerusalem's psychoanalytical circles.

Originally published in Le Monde *in May 2001, with a few editorial changes resulting from limitations on space. The complete version precedes.*

Journey through an Imperious, Wounded America

New York, 14 April 2002

The two rays of light that pierced the night in the place of the vanished towers of the World Trade Center are gone in the fading light – a final tribute. The projectors were taken apart this morning. For the twilight traveller arriving from JFK Airport, who suddenly glimpses the New York skyline before entering the tunnel to Manhattan, nothing marks the absence of the twin towers any longer, or testifies to the apocalypse: only a giant luminous panel, on the side of the highway which projects uninterruptedly, in the snap of spangled banners, the pictures of the firemen who gave their lives on 11 September.

Monday 15 April

Ground Zero. That is the name now given to this surface brought down to nothing, to zero, this *tabula rasa*. The subway's E line – the terminus is still called 'World-Trade-Center' – used to be crawling with golden boys in flashy ties, secretaries in suits and trainers, their pumps in their handbags,

Pakistani or African peddlers: New York's colourful crowd, always rushing, tense, vibrant; there are no more than ten of us leaving the underground this mid-morning. The exit looks onto the fence of Saint Paul's Chapel, Manhattan's oldest parish, alongside its English village cemetery shaded by trees where squirrels bound. This incongruous haven of bygone days, amidst the glass and steel skyscrapers, has become a spontaneous popular mausoleum where yesterday's dead welcome those of today: across the street, beyond the site's pickets, the torn bodies were evacuated among mountains of gravel. The fence of the cemetery and the church has become an immense votive wall where people have hung bunches of flowers, signs, and an incredible number of t-shirts and baseball caps inscribed with the names of sports teams or the words 'I Love NY' with the big red heart. From the futurist world of the Financial Center one plunges suddenly into a religion from the dawn of time that reminds me of the figures and marabouts around which people tie ribbons in the Orient and Africa, of those antique temples where consecrated relics were hung: an offering to the dead from a people that has spontaneously rediscovered a pious gesture, both primitive and sublime, and expressing, in the most intimate emotional register, an anguish that sticks to the skin. In the surrounding neighbourhood, hundreds of thousands of jobs have been lost; those who have been ruined and have received no indemnity are on the street, their poor belongings in a supermarket trolley. The homeless are back, after the years of prosperity during which they had almost disappeared. Street vendors are selling packets of photos and postcards of the catastrophe: towers in flames, haggard passers-by stumbling in the dust, and 'Bin Laden Wanted' for five million dollars, like the posters in Westerns – as if to ward off the mind-boggling terrorism of 11 September through the familiar icon of a Wild West outlaw.

The same day in Washington, the largest pro-Israeli demonstration in US history gathers a hundred thousand Jews and representatives of the fundamentalist Christian Right on the Mall, in front of the White House, just as Secretary of State Colin Powell, on a Middle East tour, is meeting Arafat in Ramallah. The demonstrators call the Palestinian leader a terrorist and boo the assistant secretary of defence, Paul Wolfowitz, although he is one of the administration's hawks – dispatched by President Bush to maintain contact with these precious voters and their powerful lobby. Having reiterated the US's support for the Hebrew State, Mr Wolfowitz mentioned Palestinian suffering, and the crowd was having none of it. Now 11 September is the only lens through which America sees the world; Sharon's partisans have been quick to recycle the logic of the war on terror for their own benefit. The Arabs, because of the suicide bombings inside Israel, run the risk of losing the image war in America.

16 April

Today a tape shown on al-Jazeera is being aired on television. For the first time, one of the hijackers, the Saudi Arabian Ahmad al-Haznawi, is claiming responsibility for the attacks in Bin Laden's name, in a sort of pre-recorded will. While he is reading his statement, a clumsy photomontage shows the twin towers in flames on the left of the screen, while the Arabic words wink: 'Chase out the infidels (*mushrikin*) from the Arabian Peninsula' – a saying of the Prophet Muhammad that Bin Laden has taken as his slogan. Clips of him and his sidekick al-Zawahiri are inserted regularly: they are calling for *jihad*, as is their wont, but say nothing of the situation in Palestine, or the siege of Jenin – which the Arabs want to have recognized by the international community as a massacre of civilians: a genocide.

The victim's status is a major stake in the war of symbolic images and poses: it allows one to mark the adversary with the stigma of terrorism. A very widespread rumour in the Arab world holds that the Israeli Mossad is in fact behind the attacks, and that most of the dead are Muslim. By claiming responsibility explicitly for the carnage in New York and Washington on behalf of Bin Laden and a few allied henchmen, the tape being shown today adduces the missing proof of their implication. Why suddenly ruin the logic of doubt and victimization? At the moment of the Jenin drama, it is crucial for Bin Laden, his sponsors and his followers that his icon appear in the media: by attributing responsibility for 11

September to him officially, he is proclaimed the avenger of all Arab suffering, past and present, in the name of the *lex talionis*; he is reinstated at the centre of the Middle East's political and military stakes. Yet nothing on the tape proves that Bin Laden is still alive: the images of him appear dated. Have his supporters been galvanized, their ranks swollen – or has the horror he inspires been confirmed, and mingled a little more closely with the Palestinian cause in American minds?

17 April

At Columbia University, one of the best known in the country and one of the centres of confrontation in 1968, posters call for a demonstration in solidarity with Palestine on the occasion of the assault on Jenin and Arafat's imprisonment in his Ramallah headquarters. It brings together only a few dozen students in an atmosphere of general incomprehension, to say the least. A colleague wonders what has become of students' capacity to critique received wisdom: after the shock of 11 September, it is almost unthinkable to question the Manichaean dichotomy of the 'war on terror', with its black-and-white worldview, 'good guys' against 'bad guys', for which the Palestinians are paying the price.

18 April

Washington. Richard Perle is head of the Pentagon's Policy Advisory Board, the body that elaborates the ideas that matter in the Defence Department. Under Ronald Reagan, he was one of the USSR's most implacable enemies and from that time has preserved the nickname 'Prince of Darkness', which this affable man humourously claims as his own. He recounted his struggle, scarcely romanticized at all, in a very successful thriller titled *Hard Line*, in which real-life characters were given fictional names. The same hard line that caused the Soviets' defeat will bring about the downfall of America's enemies in the Middle East. In that sense, George W. Bush is as much Reagan's direct heir as he is his father's son – and today's 'Axis of Evil' is the offspring of yesterday's 'Evil Empire'. For the hardliners in the Defence Department, evicting Saddam Hussein is the only rational option for freeing up the situation in the region and triggering a virtuous circle of American-style reform and modernization that will break the vicious circle of terrorism, dictatorship and poverty.

The Israeli-Palestinian peace process has done its time; the conflict in the Holy Land is inextricable and US intervention between Sharon and Arafat impossible. It is necessary to deal with the Middle East question holistically: once Saddam has been eliminated and replaced by a pro-American regime, Iraq will return to its place as a regional power and major petrol producer. Saudi Arabia will see its hegemony over this market threatened by a modern state where middle classes will emerge, trustworthier than the tribal monarchy of which most of the 11 September terrorists were subjects. The domino effect of a pro-

American Iraq will allow the Middle East as a whole, including Israel, to hop on the train of prosperous globalization, which will relativize territorial, national or religious conflicts.

While accepting the ideological coherence of such a vision – without political or moral prejudice – I wonder about certain practical aspects; will the region's states, Saudi Arabia foremost among them, remain passive against an offensive that threatens their interests? Are the Iraqi middle classes, annihilated by the US-led embargo, ready to throw themselves into Washington's arms? The heralds of the war against Saddam send the Cassandras back to the Taliban's hasty rout, the rejoicing of Kabul's inhabitants in November 2001 – this, they say, is but a poor harbinger of the elation that will prevail in Baghdad, to be liberated by the end of the year. I am surprised, during my conversations with the 'hardliners', by their certainty that Arab societies are as culturally estranged from the regimes that lead them as the Poles or Hungarians were from Communist ideology. They are convinced that eliminating Saddam will automatically bring the region's peoples into the victor's camp, that the virulent anti-Americanism of the 'Arab street' is an empty theory that a few well-targeted missiles will sweep away, a chimera that aspirations for prosperity will soon dispel.

In the past ten years or so, American universities have hardly accumulated any knowledge at all about the Middle East, where, after Oslo, peace was believed to be close at hand but where investment perspectives were judged mediocre. It was no twice as many American flags and 'We Love America' stickers hung in his cabin than his average colleague. A heat wave has hit the East Coast and he is wearing shorts – rarely the outfit of a fanatical Islamist – but how can one tell, since the 11 September hijackers disguised themselves as trendy youngsters to avert suspicion? We begin to talk; he is Syrian, and delighted to chat in Damascene dialect. He came to America because he could no longer bear the religious pressure on his daily life. He says he is secular; he married a Slovak and sought the anonymous freedom of a Western metropolis. Since the attacks, he has been locked once again in the identity he attempted to escape through emigration. He despises Bin Laden and everything he represents, and this forces him to deck his taxi out in star-spangled banners, as if to apologize for existing.

20 April

On a wall of Saint-Vincent's Hospital, the biggest of those close to the twin towers, a piece of the mosaic of little signs that covered the city after 11 September has been preserved under glass. 'They were everywhere,' explains Richard, a friend who works as a nurse: 'On every lamppost, every wall, every letterbox, with *Missing* written in big letters, and a picture of the disappeared. People always hoped that their loved one would be found – and finally the rain and wind got to these pieces of paper; you could see them fluttering, attached by a piece of tape, before a gust blew them away.' The missing appear in candid shots, holding a beer, in the kitchen or on the beach – sometimes they are wearing a suit, a tie and a smile. By the infinite variety in skin colour, features and the origins of their names, one can measure as never before that New York is the universe's cosmopolitan capital – and that a crime against humanity, against humans in all their diversity, has been committed. Richard is still traumatized by the attacks. He lives alone; his friend died of AIDS a few years ago. 'What I don't like,' he says, 'is all the fake patriotism, the recycling by the religious Right. As if they were taking over exclusive representation of the dead.'

In Washington, a coalition of anti-globalization and pro-Palestinian activists is demonstrating in front of the White House, in reply to Monday's Israel supporters. This is the first time since 11 September that Arab Americans have raised their voices collectively – Jenin's destruction allows them to do so. Veiled students are being interviewed on television and accusing Israel, calling it a terrorist state. A Moroccan American friend who supports the Palestinians explains why she refuses to be represented by the Islamists, who are trying to speak in the name of the community as a whole, and who monopolize screens and microphones – just as the hawks, on the other side, seized the Jewish word.

21 April
Boston. The receptionist at the hotel is named Mujahid –

literally, 'the Jihad soldier'. A nuclear physics engineer originally from Bab al-Oued, he fled Algeria in 1997 (the year the great massacres took place and the GIA was dissolved) and found refuge for his family in the US. His French pronunciation is eroded by Arabic and English: he has just seen on television that 'Le Pan' would run against Chirac in the second round of the French presidential elections. He wonders if the Arabs will have to leave France.

22 April

Harvard, the Faculty Club. Professor Huntington, author of *The Clash of Civilizations*, seems surprised when I tell him that his book, of which the Arabic translation is a bestseller, is the top reference for all Islamist militants, thrilled by the cultural rift that gives credence to their confrontational ideology. All they have to do is invert the signs of Good and Evil to set themselves up as champions of the cause for all Arabs and Muslims combined, against a West it is now easy for them to demonize.

23 April

Zacarias Abbas Moussaoui would tend to bear out Professor Huntington's theses. This French citizen of Moroccan origin, arrested shortly before 11 September and suspected of having been the potential twentieth hijacker, is in prison in Virginia and could face execution for conspiracy. He has refused visits from any French consular representative. His battle is elsewhere, with God, Who he prays will destroy America, the Jews and their state. He is on all the front pages: he has declined the court-appointed attorneys because they are not Muslim, and wants to defend himself – unless the court grants him an attorney of his religion, at the American taxpayer's expense. If he argues his case, he will have access to confidential documents: US security could be threatened. If he obtains the lawyer he is demanding, jurisprudence will subsequently allow defendants – whether white, black, women, gay – to insist on representation by a member of their community, ethnic group or gender, and refuse all other attorneys. On the *New York Times*'s op-ed pages, a law professor suggests allowing him a Muslim lawyer to ensure every possible juridical guarantee for the trial. The case looks set to be thorny: how is it possible to justify the requisite death penalty for a defendant who, although he trumpets his hatred for America and the Jews, has killed no one himself?

25 April

President Bush has invited Prince Abdallah, the heir to the Saudi Arabian throne and the kingdom's strongman, to his ranch in Crawford, Texas. Only Vladimir Putin, master of the Kremlin, and Tony Blair, that unshakeable ally, have enjoyed such a mark of distinction. It indicates the crucial importance still granted to relations with the West's main petrol supplier: today, the prince is indeed the only one who can make the president hear an Arab voice. Yet fifteen Saudis were among the 11 September hijackers, and – to the great chagrin of American commentators – a telethon in the kingdom has just raised large sums of money for the families of Palestinian 'martyrs' killed on suicide missions in Israel. Against the hawks in Defence and Congress, whose leaders reiterate their unshakeable support for Israel during the prince's visit to Texas, the pragmatists emphasize that the US cannot run the risk of destabilization in Saudi Arabia, which would ignite oil prices and create an earthquake in the global economy: the Saudi and the Texan have no other choice beyond the narrow path of their mutual interest.

27 April

Los Angeles. The person I am speaking to, in one of those producers' villas nestled in the luxuriant vegetation off Mulholland Drive, does not hesitate to say that 11 September has disrupted the film industry profoundly. The images of the burning twin towers seemed to come straight out of a disaster blockbuster. Suddenly, Hollywood cinema, having fed pop culture worldwide on its inventions, had lent its language to a monstrous reality that was turning against America. Screenplays along those lines were judged inappropriate and all projects were postponed, as though to disprove any link between the movie industry and the terrorist activities moulded in its image to increase their symbolic impact on the planet's television audiences.

Some directors want to pay tribute to the victims of 11 September, based on accounts of the thousands of shattered lives the press has covered. But the endeavour could not provide an opportunity for financial profit, and so nothing is being done, since moral exigencies and production costs pull in opposite directions. Others have tried to build bridges between the rather democratic, liberated world of cinema and the conservative, moralistic Republicans in the White House to make patriotic movies – more dead ends. Hollywood, beyond the standardized products of the dream machine, has always given America sublime inventions that treated its historical traumas through the catharsis of passion and drama. How many years will have to pass before the studios can face the horror of 11 September in its global dimension, before Hollywood can overcome its immense distress and transcend, in its own words, the greatest challenge that imperious, wounded America has ever known?

Originally published in Le Monde *in May 2002.*

Index